P[illegible]S
Islâmic Rights & Responsibilities

M. M. Ashiq Ilahi Bulandshehri (Ra)

www.idaraimpex.com

PARENTS ISLĀMIC RIGHTS & RESPONSIBILITIES

M. M. Ashiq Ilahi Bulandshehri (Ra)

9 788171 015023 00000

ISBN 81-7101-502-6

Edition 2011

TP-050-11

Published by Mohammad Yunus for
IDARA IMPEX
D-80, Abul Fazal Enclave-I, Jamia Nagar
New Delhi-110 025 (India)
Tel.: 2695 6832 Fax: +91-11-6617 3545
Email: **sales@idaraimpex.com**
Visit us at: **www.idarastore.com**

Designed & Printed in India

Typesetted at: **DTP Division**
IDARA ISHA'AT-E-DINIYAT
P.O. Box 9795, Jamia Nagar, New Delhi-110025 (India)

CONTENTS

Chapter 3

Chapter 4

Chapter 5

PUBLISHER'S NOTE

The books written by *Maulana Ashiq Ilahi Bulandshehri*, are a notable contribution to the constructive literature that has proved very fruitful in the religious guidance of Muslims.

In the present essay, the author dwells not only on the rights of parents but also on their responsibilities; as well as the rights and responsibilities of other relatives, the blessings ensuing upon obedience and fulfilment of duties due to them, and the evil consequences of their disregard, in the light of the Qur'ãn and authentic Traditions of the Holy Prophet ﷺ.

Because of the influence of Western culture and ignorance of the teachings of Islam, the rights of fellow human beings, particularly of parents, are all but forgotten. Muslim society is getting farther and farther away from the principles of Islamic social values because of its unfamiliarity with the rights that parents have on their children, the rights the children have on their parents and those of other relatives. Day by day the horrid results of this straying away are becoming more and more glaring.

The revered author has quoted profusely the relevant passages from the Qur'ãn and the Traditions, adding his own commentary to them in a lucid style and language easy to understand.

The Urdu version has been brought out by several publishers, but in view of the rapid expansion of Islam in the West, an English translation was considered indispensable. The present booklet is intended to fill the gap. May Allah bestow on it His blessings of acceptance!

Saud Ashraf Usmani

INTRODUCTION

بسم الله الرحمن الرحيم

الحمد لله وكفى وسلام على عباده الذين اصطفى

Foremost in the truth and guidance the Prophet ﷺ brought to this world, was the invitation to belief in the Divine Being. Next, he gave those who believed, certain counsels of guidance for their day to day life. These counsels may basically be divided in two sections: one, those concerning the rights Allah the Creator has on His creatures, what their duties are in respect of these Divine rights and what they should do in fulfilment of them.

The other section comprises what are called *Huqooq-ul-Ibaad* or the rights human beings have on one another; how they are to conduct themselves, not only in respect of one another, but also in respect of other creatures, and what Allah's commands are in respect of both.

The subject is of great importance. Allah has ordained that the subject of any violation of human rights, any cruelty or excesses committed must be resolved by human beings amongst themselves. Allah, Who is Compassionate and Merciful, has not assumed to Himself the forgiveness for such a crime or absolving anyone of it. Instead, He has decreed that the violator of a human right, the criminal or tyrant, must obtain the forgiveness of his victim or somehow compensate for it to the satisfaction of the victim. If neither of these is done, compensation will have to be made in the Hereafter, and compensation then will be very dear, the punishment extremely painful, as spelt out in great detail in the Qur'ãn and the Traditions.

Among the social rights, *Huqooq-ul-Ibaad*, the first priority is given to parents. A study of the Qur'ãn shows that commands for parental rights, filial service to the parents and making life pleasant for them are stated alongside those in respect of Divine Unity and devotion to the Divine Being. This means that such service and filial devotion is of importance next only to devotion to Allah. *Surah Asra*, also known as *Surah Banu Israel*, has these words:

وَقَضَىٰ رَبُّكَ أَلَّا تَعْبُدُوٓا۟ إِلَّآ إِيَّاهُ وَبِٱلْوَٰلِدَيْنِ إِحْسَـٰنًا

"And the absolute command of your Lord is that you worship none save Allah and that you treat your parents with handsome treatment." [17:23]

And in *Surah Luqman* that if the parents by any chance are pagans, their offspring must not follow their example however much they may try to induce the offspring, yet, the offspring must treat them well.

وَإِن جَـٰهَدَاكَ عَلَىٰٓ أَن تُشْرِكَ بِى مَا لَيْسَ لَكَ بِهِۦ عِلْمٌ فَلَا تُطِعْهُمَا
وَصَاحِبْهُمَا فِى ٱلدُّنْيَا مَعْرُوفًا

Whatever the Prophet ﷺ has said about the rights of parents and duties of the children towards them are, in fact, only by way of expatiating on these words of the Qur'ãn.

He once said, "Allah's consent lies in the consent of the father, and Allah's anger in the anger of the father." [*Tirmidhi*]

This means that he who wishes that his Lord Allah be happy with him should keep his father happy with him. He who does not keep his father happy he will be deprived of Allah's approbation.

In this Tradition the word used is 'father'. In the other Tradition, the 'mother' has been given precedence, as will be found in the pages of this work.

The obligations under which the child is brought up, the pains taken by the parents in bringing him up are well known. He who does not fulfil these rights and puts the parents to any suffering, in reality deprives himself of the treasure of Islam.

In these times of western dominance when the day to day life is completely upset and Islamic values are being trampled, we often hear of instances of parental rights being not merely denied but of such brutal treatment of parents as make us tremble. My leader and my teacher, the revered *Shaikh-ul-Hadith*, Maulana Muhammad Zakariya who guides many wandering souls today and embalms many a tortured one, constantly receives letters or verbal complaints of gruesome violation of parental rights. He, therefore, instructed his disciple, Maulana Ashiq Ilahi Bulandshehri, already an author of several books and booklets and who has taught hadith and *Fiqah* for a long time, and possesses indepth knowledge of Islamic literature, to write on this subject as well.

The work when completed was shown to Maulana Muhammad Zakariya who, incidentally, happened to be in Madinah these days. The work, thus, has his blessing also.

We pray to Allah that the author may be best compensated by Him and that the readers of this work may benefit increasingly by it.

Taqiuddin Nadwi Mazahiri
Madina Munawwara

PREFACE

بسم الله الرحمن الرحيم

اَلْحَمْدُ لِلّٰهِ رَبِّ الْعٰلَمِيْنَ، وَالصَّلٰوةُ وَالسَّلَامُ عَلٰى سَيِّدِنَا وَسَنَدِنَا مُحَمَّدٍ
وَاٰلِهٖ وَاَصْحَابِهٖ اَجْمَعِيْنَ۔

I have written this booklet on instructions from my spiritual leader and tutor *Shaikh-ul-Hadith* Hazrat Muhammad Zakariya. The work is a collection of those verses of the Qur'ãn and quotations from the Traditions of the Holy Prophet ﷺ, duly translated and explained, which relate to the rights of the parents and the reverence and duties and obedience owed to them; their blessings and benefits as well as the punishment consequential upon violation of parental rights, disobedience and harassment.

The booklet contains five sections:

- in the first are verses of the Qur'ãn, together with their translation and commentary;
- in the second, relevant Traditions and blessings accruing from good treatment of parents;
- in the third , the various punishments for disobedience of

parents or harassing them;

- in the fourth, the various deeds which can be done to invoke Allah's mercy on them;
- in the fifth, handsome treatment of relatives other than parents and its benefits, and the harmful results of neglecting them.

The work concludes with abbreviated quotations from Maulana Ashraf Ali Thanvi's writings on the subject.

I have presented the work in very simple, lucid Urdu. It was read out to my spiritual leader who himself arranged for its publishing.

It is requested that in order to make the work popular and widely accepted, my readers pray for the elevation of my leader, and also for my salvation, my parents and my teachers. May the shadow of my spiritual leader be on us sinners for long, and may we be blessed with the urge to benefit from his blessings.

انه مجيب الدعوات، ومفيض الجود والبركات، وبعزته وجلالته تتم الصالحات، سبحان ربك رب العزت عما يصفون. وسلام على المرسلين، والحمد لله رب العالمين.

Muhammad Ashiq Ilahi Bulandshehri

Madinah Munawwarah

Jamadi-ul-Ula, 1397 A.H.

بسم الله الرحمن الرحيم

Chapter : 1

RIGHTS AND RESPONSIBILITIES OF PARENTS

وَقَضَىٰ رَبُّكَ أَلَّا تَعْبُدُوٓاْ إِلَّآ إِيَّاهُ وَبِٱلْوَٰلِدَيْنِ إِحْسَٰنًا ۚ إِمَّا يَبْلُغَنَّ عِندَكَ
ٱلْكِبَرَ أَحَدُهُمَآ أَوْ كِلَاهُمَا فَلَا تَقُل لَّهُمَآ أُفٍّ وَلَا تَنْهَرْهُمَا وَقُل لَّهُمَا
قَوْلًا كَرِيمًا ﴿٢٣﴾ وَٱخْفِضْ لَهُمَا جَنَاحَ ٱلذُّلِّ مِنَ ٱلرَّحْمَةِ وَقُل رَّبِّ
ٱرْحَمْهُمَا كَمَا رَبَّيَانِى صَغِيرًا ﴿٢٤﴾ رَّبُّكُمْ أَعْلَمُ بِمَا فِى نُفُوسِكُمْ ۚ إِن تَكُونُواْ
صَٰلِحِينَ فَإِنَّهُۥ كَانَ لِلْأَوَّٰبِينَ غَفُورًا ﴿٢٥﴾

> "Thy lord has commanded that you worship none save Him; that you treat your parents in excellent manner. If one or both of them attain old age with you, do not say *uff* to them, nor rebuke them, but speak to them with gracious words. And lower to them the wing of submission through compassion, and say, 'my Lord! have mercy on them both as they did care for me when I was young'." [*Surah Bani Israel* 17:23-25]

In this verse the Lord the Glorious, has commanded foremost that ' you shall not worship any besides Him.' This is the basic command common to all the Prophets and Messengers sent by Allah to this world; that they teach obedience to the commands given in His Books. To be firm in the faith that Allah is one, to worship none save Him, to associate none as partner in His Being, or in His attributes, or in the reverence due to Him, or in His teachings.

Allah is the Creator Who has given us everything. Obedience and gratitude to Him are necessary at all times, and since he made parentage the medium of our coming into existence, and parents go through considerable toil and anxiety for raising us up, therefore, together with the command for worshipping Him, He has also commanded that they be honoured and treated well. This is stipulated in a number of places in the Qur'ãn. In *Surah Baqra*:

وَإِذْ أَخَذْنَا مِيثَٰقَ بَنِىٓ إِسْرَٰٓءِيلَ لَا تَعْبُدُونَ إِلَّا ٱللَّهَ وَبِٱلْوَٰلِدَيْنِ إِحْسَانًا

"And remember the time when we took a covenant from the Children of Israel that they worship none save Allah and that they respect their parents."

[2:83]

In *Al-Nisa*:

وَٱعْبُدُوا۟ ٱللَّهَ وَلَا تُشْرِكُوا۟ بِهِۦ شَيْـًٔا ۖ وَبِٱلْوَٰلِدَيْنِ إِحْسَٰنًا

"Worship Allah, associate none as partners with Him, and treat your parents well." [4:36]

In *Al-An'am*:

قُلْ تَعَالَوْا۟ أَتْلُ مَا حَرَّمَ رَبُّكُمْ عَلَيْكُمْ ۖ أَلَّا تُشْرِكُوا۟ بِهِۦ شَيْـًٔا ۖ
وَبِٱلْوَٰلِدَيْنِ إِحْسَٰنًا ۖ

"Say, come, I well recite those commands which Allah has decreed for you: that you associate nothing as partners with Him and that you treat your parents with graciousness." [6:151]

In these verses together with the proper treatment of parents, some relevant counsels are also given .

First that we must not say even uff to either of them. That is, not a word is to be spoken that may belittle the respect we owe them, or is likely to injure their feelings.

The Arabic *uff*[1] is used here as an example. "Do not say even 'oh' on any occasion," such as may be addressed to them.

Imam Hasan ﷺ, says that if there were a smaller word of disrespect than uff Allah would have forbidden that too.

[*Dur-e-Mansoor an Al-Daylami*]

Honouring parents and obedience to them, whether old or young, are always binding on the children; but old age is specifically mentioned because at that period of life, a parent is inclined to become peevish and touchy, or more susceptible to any of a variety of diseases; and the children might have to wash their basins and dirty linen, and out of boredom or disgust they might lose their patience and find it difficult to prevent words of annoyance from escaping their lips. Under such strain, to refrain from the slightest disrespect or a word that may offend the parent's feelings, is a very great thing. But many break down.

Hazrat Mujahid comments, "do not say *uff* when you wash their linen or clean up their excrete, just as they spoke no such word when they did similar things for you when you were an infant."

After forbidding the use even of the word *uff*, it is added that you say nothing unpleasant to them or rebuke them. It may be asked that since *uff*, is forbidden, how can rebuking or other stronger exclamation be correct? This is done for the sake of emphasis and further clarification.

1. M.M. Pickthall, in his translation "the Glorious Qur'ãn" has wrongly translated the word as fie, which is a very strong word of contempt in idiomatic English. The more appropriate word for *uff* would be the exclamation. '*oh*!' (*Translator*)

The words," speak to them words of graciousness," imply that the tone of speech should be soft and gentle and every demeanour expressive of courtesy and consideration.

Zubair bin Muhammad, commenting on the phrase قَوْلاً كَرِيمًا (*qaulan karima*) "gracious words", says:

إذا دعواك فقل لبيكما وسعديكما

> "This implies that if the parents call you, you should respond by answering, 'here I am present for your order to obey'."

Qatada says that the phrase قولا لينا سهلا implies softness of tone and speech and easily understandable words.

Saeed bin al-Musayyab comments that speech should be in tone and language such as that of a slave in the presence of his master who is stern and harsh, if the implications of the phrase qaulan karima are to be satisfied.

The meaning of the words وَاخْفِضْ لَهُمَا جَنَاحَ الذُّلِّ مِنَ الرَّحْمَةِ (*wakhfiz lahuma janahaz-zulla min-a-rahmate*), "and lower the wing to them in compassion", is to bow the head before them in humility and affection. Urwah, commenting, says that the phrase includes the habituating of one's self to ways that cause no difference to carrying out the heartiest desires of the parents.

Ata bin Abi Rabah commenting adds that when you speak with your parents, do not even raise and lower your hands, as you do when talking with others.

Zubair bin Muhammad further adds that if parents reviles you or even use abusive language, you should, in reply, only say, "may Allah have mercy on you."

The fourth advice given is, keep praying for your parents in the words:

رَبِّ ارْحَمْهُمَا كَمَا رَبَّيَانِى صَغِيرًا۔

"Lord! keep them both in Thy mercy, for they brought me up well when I was young."

There is the time when the child stands in need of everything, is helpless and weak and of immature intelligence and the parents look after it, suffer and take a lot of pains for its sake. Then comes a time, perhaps, fifty or sixty years later, when the position is reversed. The parents are dependent on others for their expenses and service, and the offspring is earning and has the household to take care of : it should not, remembering its own days of helplessness, grudge spending on the parents, and leave no pains for carrying out their wishes; and pray for them in gratitude thus, "Lord have mercy on them both as they brought me up when I was small."

We have in Ibne Kaseer that a man carrying his mother on his back to make the rounds of the Kaba asked the Prophet ﷺ whether he had not fulfilled his duty to her. The Prophet ﷺ replied, " not even one breath of the duty owed to her has been fulfilled!"

[*Ibn Kaseer*: Vol. 3]

Bukhari has recorded in his Al-Adab-ul-Mufrad that Abu Hurairah used to live in one house and his mother in another. Whenever he went out of his house, he would knock at his mother's door and call out:

اَلسَّلَامُ عَلَيْكَ يَا اُمَّتَاهُ وَرَحْمَةُ اللهِ وَبَرَكَاتُهُ!

(*Assalam-u-alaika ya ummatahu wa rahmat Allah wa barakatu-hu*!)

Peace be on you, mother, and Allah's mercy and His blessings!

And his mother would reply:

وَعَلَيْكَ يَا بُنَيَّ

(*Wa alaika ya bunayya*)

"And the same to you , my son."

Then Abu Hurairah would say:

رحمك الله كما ربيتني صغيرا.

May Allah's mercy be on you as you brought me up when I was small."

His mother would now say:

رحمك الله كما بررتني كبيرا.

"Allah's mercy be on you as you have treated me so well when you are grown up."

A Warning

If sometime there should be any lapse in obedience or courtesy to the parents, it is the son's or daughter's duty immediately to beseech their pardon and make them happy, and at the same time pray for Allah's forgiveness.

Saeed bin Jabir commenting on the verse," your Lord knows what is in your breasts, " says that Allah forgives if there is any lapse of courtesy as such to parents, if the will to obedience to them is present in the heart. ”

Prayer for forgiveness of unbelieving parents in not permissible, but if they are living, prayers for their guidance are commendable. The relevant words in Surah Luqman are:

وَوَصَّيْنَا ٱلْإِنسَـٰنَ بِوَٰلِدَيْهِ حَمَلَتْهُ أُمُّهُۥ وَهْنًا عَلَىٰ وَهْنٍ وَفِصَـٰلُهُۥ فِى
عَامَيْنِ أَنِ ٱشْكُرْ لِى وَلِوَٰلِدَيْكَ إِلَىَّ ٱلْمَصِيرُ ﴿١٤﴾ وَإِن جَـٰهَدَاكَ
عَلَىٰٓ أَن تُشْرِكَ بِى مَا لَيْسَ لَكَ بِهِۦ عِلْمٌ فَلَا تُطِعْهُمَا
وَصَاحِبْهُمَا فِى ٱلدُّنْيَا مَعْرُوفًا وَٱتَّبِعْ سَبِيلَ مَنْ أَنَابَ إِلَىَّ ثُمَّ

إِلَيَّ مَرْجِعُكُمْ فَأُنَبِّئُكُم بِمَا كُنتُمْ تَعْمَلُونَ ﴿١٥﴾

"And We have enjoined upon man concerning his parents-his mother beareth him in weakness upon weakness and his weaning is in two years-give thanks unto Me and unto the parents. But if they strive to make thee ascribe unto as partners that of which thou hast no knowledge, then obey them not. Consort with them in the words kindly, and follow the path of him who repenteth unto Me. Then unto Me will be your return, and I shall tell you what you used to do." [31:14-15]

We note that Allah has prescribed important principle of behaviour towards parents, also reminding us of the pains they go through for our sake. The greatest suffering is borne by the mother, who grows weaker during the pregnancy, and puts with her condition with courage. Then there are the pangs of childbirth which cause her immense pain, referred to in Surah Ahqaf as:

حَمَلَتْهُ أُمُّهُ كُرْهًا وَوَضَعَتْهُ كُرْهًا

(*hamalat-hu ummo-hu kurhan wa- wadha'at -hu kurhan*).

His mother carried him with hardship and gave birth to him with hardship [46:15]

This is followed by the fostering, nursing, keeping the infant close to her bosom through winter and summer. If it falls ill, the parents forget their sleep; keep sitting with it in their lap; pay repeated visits to the doctor; if the clothes are messed up, they bear it all with all pleasantness, wash the bed linen, and so on. Evidently, this labour and love should be repaid with gratitude.

Our utmost gratitude is due to Allah the Glorious who gave us our existence; next gratitude is to our parents who fostered us and brought us up and suffered for us. This is what Allah has commanded in the words:

أَنِ ٱشْكُرْ لِى وَلِوَٰلِدَيْكَ

(*An-i-shkur-li wa liwa-lidaika*)

"Thank me and your parents." [31:14]

Just as gratitude to Allah is not complete by mere utterance of words but by obedience to every commandment of Allah, similarly, it is not enough to express gratitude to parents in so many words or by praising them or acknowledging their pains, but by obedience, keeping away from disobedience, and spending on them by labour and of wealth.

Someone asked Imam Hasan how was one to perform good service to parents, he replied "spend of your wealth on them, carry out whatever they ask you to do unless they ask you to commit a sin, when you must not obey them." [*Durr-e-Mansoor*]

It must be kept in mind that after giving the command for gratitude to parents, it is emphasised that however great the obligation to parents might be, they are never more deserving of our gratitude than Allah is. If the parents tell one to associate partners with Allah or not merely tell one but even compel, they must not be obeyed. This is explained in *Surah Luqman*.

Besides *shirk* (association of partner with Allah, one must not obey if the parents ask their son or daughter to renounce prayers or fasting or the great pilgrimage (hajj), or to eat of what is forbidden. The Prophet ﷺ tells us.

لاَ طَاعَةَ لِمَخْلُوقٍ فِى مَعْصِيَةِ الْخَالِقِ-

"Obedience to any creature does not comprise disobedience to Creator."

Whether it be a parent, a religious leader or spiritual leader (*Peer*), teacher or government official, howsoever high, obedience to him is permissible only when it does not imply disobedience to our Lord , the Creator of all.

It is also added in Surah Luqman:

وَصَاحِبْهُمَا فِي ٱلدُّنْيَا مَعْرُوفًا ۖ

Live gracefully with the parents in this world." [31:15]

That is, if the parents are idolatrous or of evil lives, do not follow their example or obey them in such respect, but even so, there should be no difference in good treatment of them or service to them. Everyone will be given his due on the Last Day.

Good treatment in this world is not dependent on the parents being Muslim or pious. Asma, Abu Bakr's daughter, narrates, "during the period of the Hudaibiya Truce, my mother who was a *mushrik* (an idolator) came to stay with me and desired that I should help her with money. So I asked the Prophet ﷺ what I should do. He advised me to help her as she desired and be compassionate with her."

This means that assistance and merciful treatment must not be allowed to abate even if the parents be pagan. But their pagan ways or false religion must not be adopted whether they advise it or not. Sa'd bin abi Waqas tells us that the verse:

وَإِن جَٰهَدَاكَ عَلَىٰٓ أَن تُشْرِكَ بِي مَا لَيْسَ لَكَ بِهِۦ عِلْمٌ فَلَا تُطِعْهُمَا ۖ

(*Wa-in jahadaka ala an tushrika bi ma laysa laka bihi ilmun falatutihuma*)

"But if they strive to make thee ascribe partners unto Me, them obey them not." [31:15]

Was revealed with reference to him:

"What happened was that I used to treat my mother very well. When became Muslim she told me, 'Sa'd, have you adopted some new religion for yourself? Give it up: and if you do not, I will neither eat nor drink but will die of starvation, and people will taunt you that you killed me "O murderer of your mother!", they will call you.

I told her not to do this and that I would not give up my religion Islam for anything whatever. After this, she did not eat or drink the first day and she weakened: the next day again she went without food or drink and she got weaker: the third day she did the same, and got worse. I told her, " mother, even if you had a hundred lives, and every life passed away one by one, I would not go back on Islam "

After this she resumed eating and drinking." [*Ibn-e-Kaseer*: Vol. 3, p. 445 and *Muslim in Fadhail-e-Sahaba*]

We have in *Surah Ahqaf*:

وَوَصَّيْنَا ٱلْإِنسَـٰنَ بِوَٰلِدَيْهِ حَمَلَتْهُ أُمُّهُۥ وَهْنًا عَلَىٰ وَهْنٍ وَفِصَـٰلُهُۥ فِى
عَامَيْنِ أَنِ ٱشْكُرْ لِى وَلِوَٰلِدَيْكَ إِلَىَّ ٱلْمَصِيرُ ﴿١٤﴾ وَإِن جَـٰهَدَاكَ
عَلَىٰٓ أَن تُشْرِكَ بِى مَا لَيْسَ لَكَ بِهِۦ عِلْمٌ فَلَا تُطِعْهُمَا
وَصَاحِبْهُمَا فِى ٱلدُّنْيَا مَعْرُوفًا وَٱتَّبِعْ سَبِيلَ مَنْ أَنَابَ إِلَىَّ ثُمَّ
إِلَىَّ مَرْجِعُكُمْ فَأُنَبِّئُكُم بِمَا كُنتُمْ تَعْمَلُونَ ﴿١٥﴾

"And we have commanded unto mankind kindness towards parents. His mother beareth him with pain and bringeth him forth with pain and the bearing of him and the weaning of him is thirty months, till when he attaineth full strength and reacheth forty years, he sayeth, 'my Lord! arouse me that I may give thanks for the favour wherewith Thou hast favoured me and my parents and that I may do right acceptable unto Thee. And be gracious unto me in matter of my seed. Lo! I am of those who surrender (unto Thee).

Those are they from whom we accept the best of what they do and overlook their evil deeds, They are among the owners of the Garden. This is the true promise which they were promised (in the world.

[46:15-16]

Blessed is he who renders unto Allah the rights due to Allah and to parents the rights due to the parents and thanks Allah for the blessings He has bestowed on him and also for those blessings which He has bestowed on his parents, because the parents are also a media of blessing and the blessings bestowed on them are transferred to their children.

Chapter : 2

BENEFITS AND REWARDS OF DEVOTION TO PARENTS

عَنْ اِبْنِ مَسْعُوْد رَضِىَ اللهُ عَنْهُ قَالَ سَاَلْتُ النَبِىُّ صَلَّى اللهُ عَلَيْهِ وَسَلَّمْ:
اَىُّ الْاَعْمَالُ اَحُبُّ اِلَى اللهِ؟ قَالَ النَبِىُّ، اَلصَّلٰوةُ لِوَقْتِهَا' قُلْتُ: ثُمَّ اَىُّ؟
قَالَ: "اَلْبِرُّ الْوَالِدَيْنِ" قُلْتُ ثُمَّ اَىُّ؟ قَالَ: اَلْجِهَادُ فِىْ سَبِيْلِ اللهِ". قَالَ
حَدَّثْنِىْ بهن، وَلَوْ اِسْتَزَدْتُهٗ لزادنى۔ (رواه البخاری)

A Tradition from Abdullah bin Masud, رضي الله عنه narrates, "I asked the Prophet ﷺ, *what* deed was most loved by Allah, and he replied, ' to offer prayers (*Salãt*) at the right times.'

"And next?, I asked.

He said, ' to treat your parents well.'

'And next again? 'I persisted, and he said, ' to strive (*jihad*) in Allah's path'.

Masud adds, "this is what the Prophet ﷺ said in answer to my questions, and if I had asked him any more questions, he would have continued answering me. " [*Bukhari and Muslim in Mishkat-ul-Masabih*]

We note that the deed Allah loves most is that prayers be offered to Him within the times stipulated, next , the best treatment of parents, and after this, *jihad.* This means that the blessings of doing good to parents, i.e., treating parents well are greater than those of *jihad.*

In various Traditions treating parents well has been equalled with rights, and the same words are used for treatment of other relatives as well.

In Arabic, the word is used for good treatment, and *Haqooque* for causing pain, offending feelings, disobedience, and such.

Mulla Ali Qari writes in his commentary on the *Mishkat-al Masabih* that bir is *Ihsãn* or handsome treatment, the word being used for such treatment of parents as well as other relatives. The antonym is aqooque, maltreatment of parents and other relatives and violating their rights.

Besides bir and aqooque there are two other words, rather phrases. صلة الرحم *Sira-tul-Raham* and قطيعة ارحم *Qatia-tul-Raham*, by way of compassion and sympathy with blood relative and turning away from such compassion and sympathy, respectively. Mulla Ali Qari comments that *Sila-tul-Raham* is good treatment of blood relatives and of the in-laws, to be concerned with their welfare, and such, while *Qatia-tul-Raham* is quite the opposite. He who does *Sila-tul-Raham* strengthens the joint of relationship that exists between one and another relative, *Sila* is from the root *wasl* or 'joining' , and he who treats the relatives badly, breaks and disrupts the joint; disjoins, in a word. Literally, 'cuts off the relationship.

MOTHER HAS PRECEDENCE

عن ابى هريرة رضى الله عنه، قال: قال رجل: يا رسول الله صلى الله عليه وسلم من احق بحسن صحابتى؟ قال: امك. قال ثم من؟ قال:

امك قال ثم من؟ قال: امك۔ قال: ثم من؟ قال ابوك وفى رواية/قال:
امك۔ ثم امك ثم امك ثم اباك ثم ادناك ثم ادناك۔

It is recorded in the Traditions on the authority of Abu Hurairah, that a man asked the Prophet ﷺ who had the most priority to good treatment. The Prophet ﷺ answered,' your mother."

The man asked, "and next to mother?"

The Prophet ﷺ said, " your mother."

"And next, again asked the man.

"Your mother, "replied the Prophet ﷺ once more.

"And next"? the man persisted.

"Your father, "the Prophet ﷺ answered.

In another Tradition , the same sentiment is expressed but in different words. The Prophet ﷺ said three times that the mother had the first right and then the father, and after the two, the nearest relative had the right to handsome treatment, and then the next, and the next.

The mother has the first claim because she bears the child and more than anyone else goes through great toil and suffering for bringing up the child. And because she is the weaker and cannot go out to earn her own livelihood while the father can, she has the precedence for the right to better treatment.

After the parents come the rights of other relatives. Here, the grades of precedence are marked; the nearest first, and then the next nearest, and so on.

From the Traditions quoted here, some *Ulamah* have drawn the conclusion that in being treated well and with munificence, the mother has three times a greater right than the father, because she goes through three distinct stages of labour and suffering: that of the period of pregnancy; then childbirth and then nursing. The jurists or *fuqaha* further clarify that for kind treatment the mother has precedence, but for honour and courtesies the father has precedence, when the son or daughter, out of his or her solicitude to serve both equally, is unable to do so because of lack of means. (*Mazahir-e-Haq*)

PARENTS ARE MEDIAM OF PARADISE AND HELL

عن ابی امامه رضی الله عنه ان رجلا قال: یا رسول الله ما حق الوالدین علی ولدهما؟ قال هما جنتك و نارك۔

It is recorded on the authority of Ibn Majah that a man asked the Prophet ﷺ, what rights the parents had on their children, and the Prophet ﷺ answered," both are your paradise and your hell.

(*Mishkat-al-Masabih*: p 421)

That is to say, paradise is assured for those who serve their parents with love; compassion and due courtesy and spend on them according to means, but they who cause their parents suffering and pain and disobey them merit punishment in the Hereafter.

ALLAH'S PLEASURE LIES IN THE PLEASURE OF THE PARENTS

وعن عبدالله بن عمر رضی الله عنه قال: قال رسول الله صلی الله علیه وسلم: رضا الله فی رضا الوالدین، و سخط الله فی سخط الوالدین۔

(أخرجه الحاکم وصححه، والبیهقی کذا فی الدر المنثور)

Abdullah bin Umar relates that the Prophet ﷺ said, "Allah's pleasure and approval are in the pleasure and approval of the parents, and Allah's anger lies in the anger of the parents."

In other words, Allah is happy with one whom one's parents are happy with , and Allah is annoyed with one whom one's parents are annoyed with, because Allah has commanded obedience and service to parents, and disobedience of His command rouses His anger.

It should be remembered that this holds good only if the parents do not demand obedience to anything forbidden in the *shariah*. Obedience, then, will not be permissible. Should the parents be displeased, no attention should be paid to their displeasure because in such a case Allah is pleased and not displeased with the disobedience.

THE FATHER IS BEST OF DOORS TO PARADISE

عن ابی درداء رضی الله عنه قال: سمعت رسوّل الله صلی الله علیه وسلم یقول: الوالد اوسط ابواب الجنة، فاحفظ ذلك الباب اوضیعه۔

(أخرجه ابن ابی شیبة والحاکم وصححه البیهقی کذا فی الدر المنثور)

Abu Darda tells us that he heard the Prophet ﷺ say, "your father is the middle door (that is, the best of doors) to paradise . It depends on you to safeguard this door by obedience or lose it by disobedience."

(*Baihaqi*: Vol. 4)

TO LOOK AT PARENTS WITH COMPASSION IS EQUAL TO ACCEPTANCE OF THE GRAND PILGRIMAGE

عن ابن عباس رضى الله عنه أن رسول الله قال: مامن ولد بار ينظر الى والديه نظرة رحمة إلا كتب الله له بكل نظرة حجة مبرورة قالوا وان نظر كل يوم مائة مرة. قال الله اكبر اطيب.

(أخرجه البيهقى فى شعب الايمان كذا فى مشكوٰة)

It is on record on the authority of Ibn Abbas that the Prophet ﷺ said, "every time one who treats his parents handsomely, looks at them with compassion in his eyes, Allah writes for him the reward of a grand pilgrimage (hajj).

The Companions asked, " even if one looks at one's parents a hundred times in the day ? "

The Prophet ﷺ answered, "yes, Allah is very great. He gives whatever and as much as He wants to give; none can stop Him from doing whatever He wishes to do. And He is Holy, very Holy (loss and shortage are not for him).

(From Baihaqi included in *Mishkat-al-Masabih*)

In the commentary in Mansoor it is also stated on the authority of Ibn Abbas that whenever one looks at his father with a look that gladdens him, Allah assigns one the reward of freeing a slave. The Companions asked, "If one looks three hundred and sixty times in such manner ?"

The Prophet ﷺ answered, "Allah is very great (transcends loss or paucity), i.e., He is all powerful . To reward thus at every look is nothing to Him. (*Baihaqi*)

Abdullah bin Masud says that to look at the father is a prayer; to look at the Quran is a prayer; to look at one's brother whom one loves for Allah's sake is a prayer. (*Baihaqi*)

HANDSOME TREATMENT OF THE MOTHER MAKES ONE'S OWN CHILDREN TREAT ONE HANDSOMELY

عن ابى هريرة رضى الله عنه قال: قال رسول الله صلى الله عليه وسلم: عفوا عن نساء الناس تعف نسائكم وبروا آباء كم تبر كم ابناء كم ومن اتاه اخوه متنصلا فليقبل ذلك منه محقا كان او مبطلان فان لم يفعل لم يرد علي الحوض.

Abu Hurairah narrates, the Prophet ﷺ, said, "remain pure in respect of the women of other people, for, doing so, your women will remain pure; and treat your children handsomely; for, if you do so they will treat you handsomely. And should anyone come to you apologising, accept his apology, whether he is in the right or in the wrong. If you do not do so, you will not come to my *Haudh-e-Kausar* (pond of abundance).(*Mustadrak Haakim*)

Three significant points to be noted here are:

1) If you refrain from casting lewd eyes on women other than your own and do not let your lower self incline to them, the reward from Allah will be that your women will remain pure; men of lewd inclinations will not be attracted to them, nor will your women look at them with lewd eyes.

2) It is further explained that if you treat your parents well, your children will also treat you well. It hardly requires to be commented that if you behave well towards your parents, your children, who can only follow your example, are bound to treat you in the same good manner, because when they see that you honour your parents ,and that you spend of your wealth on them, they will understand that honouring parents in this manner is part of their social ethics. It will be ingrained in their minds that they, too, should honour their parents in like manner.

Going deeper into the subject, it will be appreciated that as you sow , likewise shall you reap. If you treat your parents well, Allah the Glorious will reward you by making your children inclined to treat you in a similar way, and will hold your honour, and appreciation of you in their heart.

Contrarywise it may be stated that if you treat your parents badly, your children, when their turn comes, are bound to treat you in the bad manner they remember you treated your parents.

A story goes that a man wrapped up his father in a sheet of cloth and took the bundle to throw it into a well. When he arrived there and was about to unload himself ,his father called out, "my son, throw me in some other well because this is the well I threw my father in."

Hearing these words, the man opened the bundle and took his father back home with due respect.

3) The next point explained here is that should someone do anything that annoys you or grieves you, and later he seeks your pardon, pardon him and clear your heart of all grievance. Do not think whether the fault was his or yours. Forgive as soon as forgiveness is beseeched. And if it was your fault you should also ask the other's forgiveness, and if you did anything to violate his right, do the needful to

restore the right.

A Tradition states that if one asks his brother for pardon, and the other man does not pardon him, it will be a great sin such as that of an official who realises a tax by inflicting acts of cruelty. [Baihaqi in Sha'b *Mishkat-al-Masabih*]

A FATHER'S PRAYER IS ALWAYS HEARD

و عن ابى هريرة رضى الله تعالى عنه قال: قال رسول الله صلى الله عليه وسلم: ثلاث دعوات مستجابات لاشك فيهن دعوة الوالد ودعوة المسافر ودعوة المظلوم۔

Abu Hurairah has quoted the Holy Prophet ﷺ, as saying ,"three prayers are always heard: a father's prayer for his children; a traveller's prayer; and the prayer of one who is wronged. "

(*Tirmizi, Abu Dawood, Ibn-e-Majah*)

This Tradition indicates the importance of a father's prayer. Mullah Ali Qari writes in his commentary on the Mishkat-al- Masabih that though the mother's prayer is not mentioned here in so many words, it should be understood that being the superior in precedence, her prayer, too, is accepted. The children ought to keep serving both their parents and so keep earning the blessings of their prayers and should do nothing that may offend their feelings and cause them to imprecate a harmful prayer, because just as a good prayer for the offspring's welfare is heard so also a prayer that is virtually a curse; though more often than not, because of the parents's great affection, they do not subject their offspring to a bad prayer. A parents's prayer can be both a source of blessings for the offspring and also destroy their lives in this world and the next.

وعن عائشة رضی الله تعالی عنها قالت: اتی رجل رسول الله صلی الله علیه وسلم ومعه شیخ۔ فقال: من هذا معك۔ قال: ابی قال: لا تمشي امامه ولا تقعد قبله ولا تدعه باسمه ولا تستب له۔

It is recorded on the authority of lady Ayesha that a young man accompanied by an elder called on the Prophet ﷺ. The Prophet ﷺ asked the young who the elder was." He is my father," the young man answered.

The Prophet ﷺ advised him, " always be considerate to your father and honour him. Do not walk ahead or in front of him, nor sit before he sits down, nor address him by name nor abuse anyone because of him. (*Durr-e-Mansoor*)

Honouring parents should be both by speech and by behaviour. In the Tradition quoted we note some details that comprise the concept of honouring parents.

1) It is improper to walk in front of the father and have him walk behind;

2) If it be necessary to sit, the son may do so only after the father has seated himself;

3) The son is never to address (call) his father by name but by the relationship. (That is, he should be called ' father' or 'dad', etc., or equivalent in whatever the language spoken);

4) Should anyone say something rude about your father or use an invective, do not retaliate in similar language, because such retaliation is likely to cause the man to repeat the abuse and then you become the cause for having your father abused.

We shall expatiate on this further in these pages. It is understood that these counsels are not confined in respect of the father but include the mother as well. Honouring her equally is incumbent.

HANDSOME TREATMENT OF PARENTS' AUGMENTS, AGE AND LIVELIHOOD

وعن ابی انس رضی اللہ تعالی عنہ قال: قال رسول اللہ صلی اللہ علیہ وسلم: من احب ان یمد اللہ فی عمرہ ویزید فی رزقہ فلیبر والدیہ ولیصل رحمہ۔

> Anas reports that the Prophet ﷺ said," he who desires that his life-span increases and also his means, should treat his parents magnificently and other relatives with benign compassion.. " *(Baihaqi)*

This Tradition clarifies that respectful and generous treatment of parents as well as other relatives contributes towards increasing one's years on this earth and amplifies one's means; and so also compassion and generosity with other relatives.

Further comments later:

Young men of the new generation spend lavishly on their wives and themselves but they find the very thought of spending even a penny on their parents extremely painful. Such people not only lose the reward of the Hereafter but also deprive themselves of the gains of this world. Agains that would be theirs if they had behaved better with them.

REWARD OF LABOUR TO EARN FOR PARENTS

و عن ابی عمر رضی الله تعالی عنه قال: مر رجل له جسم یعنی خلقا فقالوا: لو کان هذا فی سبیل الله. فقال النبی صلی الله علیه وسلم: لعله یکد علی صبیة صغار فهو فی سبیل الله لعله یکد علی نفسه لیغنیها عن الناس فهو فی سبیل الله.

Ibn Umar relates that when a lean thin man passed by near the Prophet's congregation of his followers, someone remarked," Ah, how good would it have been if only this man had grown lean because of striving in the path of Allah!"

The Prophet ﷺ said, "it may be that the man had become weak and emaciated because of labouring for a living for his aged parents, and that too would have been in the path of Allah; or he might have come to this condition because of labouring for his small children earning a livelihood for them, bringing them up and for their welfare, and that too would be in the path of Allah; or , perhaps, he laboured for himself, to keep his body and soul together so that he might not have to depend on others and beg for their assistance, and if so, that too would be in the path of Allah! (*Dur-e-Mansoor* From *Baihaqi*)

We find that to earn an honest livelihood for parents or children and even one's own self is included as being in the path of Allah.

BETTER THAN OPTIONAL JIHAD

وعن عبدالله بن عمر رضى الله تعالى عنهما قال: جاء رجل الى رسول الله صلى الله عليه وسلم، فاستاذنه فى الجهاد۔ فقال: احى والدك۔ قال: نعم۔ قال: ففيهما فجاهد۔

(رواه البخارى ومسلم، وفى رواية: فارجع الى والديك فاحسن صحبتهما)

We have from Abdullah bin Umar that a man came to the Prophet ﷺ ,and requested his permission to go on Jihad. The Prophet ﷺ asked the man if his parents were alive. The man replied that they were. "Then," said the Prophet ﷺ, do jihad for them." (That is , striving to earn for parents and serve them in all that they need is also a form of *jihad*).

In another version we have the words, " go back and serve your parents."

(*Bukhari and Muslim* incl. in *Mishkat-al- Masabih*)

وعن معاوية بن جاهمة رضى الله تعالىٰ عَنهما ان جاهمة رضى الله تعالىٰ عنه جاء الى النبى صلى الله عليه وسلم، فقال: يا رسول الله صلى الله عليه وسلم اردت ان اغزو وقد جئت اشتشيرك۔ فقال: هل لك من ام۔ فقال: نعم۔ قال: فالزمها، فان الجنة عند رجلها۔

Muawiyah bin Jahima reports that his father Jahima came to Prophet ﷺ and said, "It is my intention to go on jihad and have come to solicit your advice."

The Prophet ﷺ asked him whether his mother was alive and Jahima replied that she was. " Then keep yourself busy in her service because paradise lies at her feet," the Prophet ﷺ advised.

(*Ahmad, Nasai, Baihaqi* incl. in *Mishkat-al- Masabih*)

We conclude from these two ahadith that in normal conditions when *jihad* is not compulsory the virtue of serving parents is superior to optional jihad. If there is no brother or sister to serve the parents, such service becomes all the more incumbent.

Abu Saeed tells us that a man migrating from Yemen, presented himself before the Prophet ﷺ. The Prophet ﷺ said to him, "you have emigrated from the land of idolatry but still jihad is left for you to participate in. Tell me if you have left behind any relatives in Yemen."

The man replied that he had his parents there. "Have you taken their permission ?" the Prophet ﷺ asked.

"No, I have not done so", the man answered.

"Well, then, go back home. If they permit you to go on jihad, you may participate in one; otherwise stay back and continue to serve them well", the Prophet ﷺ told him. (*Ahmad in al-Hakim*)

ADVICE AT TIME OF LEAVING PARENTS IN TEARS

وعن عبدالله بن عمر رضى الله تعالى عنهما قال: جاء رجل الى النبى صلى الله عليه وسلم وصحبه وسلم يبايعه على الهجرة فقال: انى جئت ابايعك على الهجرة وتركت ابوى يبكيان۔ فقال: ارجع اليهما فاضحكهما كما ابكيتهما۔

Abdullah bin Umar reports: "a man presented himself before the Prophet ﷺ, saying that he had come to take an oath that he would migrate, and added that he had left his parents in tears because he was leaving them. The Prophet ﷺ told him to go back to them and make them smile just as he had left them in tears."

(Hakim, Abu Dawud)

This man had travelled far with laudable motives. His first motive was to emigrate; next his intention to swear on the Prophet's hand; but his parents were not agreeable that he should depart. They were thoroughly upset and wept bitterly. The Prophet ﷺ advised him to return to them and make them happy.

This explains once more how important it is to regard the feelings of the parents, to honour them and gladden their hearts.

This episode is of the time when emigrating from home was not a duty, all Arabia had converted to the new faith and everywhere Muslims could live according to the requirements of Islam.

We conclude that it is a sin to do anything that grieves, even saddens the parents; and it is a rewarding act that makes them happy and smile with joy.

According to another Tradition from Ibn Umar, the Prophet ﷺ is reported as having said that to do anything that makes the parents shed tears is one of the greater transgressions. (*Bukhari*)

Hazrat Owais Qarani was a resident of Yemen. The Prophet ﷺ called him *Khair-ul-Ta'bieen* (best of the obedient) and commanded his Companions to request Qarani to pray for them.

Owais had converted to Islam during the Prophet's life time but because of his having to remain with his mother to look after her, he could not ever visit the Prophet ﷺ, and so was not counted as a Companion, yet the Prophet ﷺ, far from finding fault with him, appreciated his staying away and in appreciation of his great worth advised his Companions to request Qarani to pray for them.

Muslim further quotes the Prophet ﷺ as saying, "Owais has a mother whom he serves well. If Owais should take an oath in Allah's name, Allah is sure to accept and fulfil his oath"

(Chapter on Virtues of Owais Qarani)

وعن عبدالله بن عمر رضى الله تعالى عنهما قال: رسول الله صلى الله عليه وسلم: لنومك على السرير بين والديك تضحكهما ويضجكانك افضل من جهادك بالسيف فى سبيل الله۔

Ibn Umar relates: the Prophet ﷺ said" your sleeping on the bed between your parents in such a way that you make them laugh with joy and they make you laugh is better than your striving with a sword in Allah's path." (*Baihaqi*)

To be happy in the eyes of the parents; to keep them happy; to make them smile; to talk with them in a manner and on topics that delight them ... are all a kind of service to them, better than jihad. This is earning a great reward for nothing.

SERVICE TO PARENTS NO LESS THAN OPTIONAL PILGRIMAGE

وعن انس رضى الله تعالى عنه اتى رجل رسول الله صلى الله عليه وسلم۔ فقال: انى اشتهى الجهاد ولا اقدر عليه فقال هل بقى احد من والديك۔ قال: امى۔ قال: قال فاتق الله فيها فاذا فعلت ذلك فانت حاج ومعتمر ومجاهد، فاذا دعتك امك فاتق الله وبرها۔

From Anas we have , a man came to the Prophet ﷺ and said ," I would like to take part in jihad but I do not possess the ability to do so."

Possibly, the man might have been physically weak, or had some defective limb. The Prophet ﷺ asked him whether his parents were still living. The man said that his mother was alive.

"Then, the Prophet ﷺ said," fear Allah in respect of your mother." (That is, devote yourself to her service.) When you do so you will have performed the pilgrimages of hajj and *Umrah* and also jihad; and when your mother calls you, fear Allah (by responding to her voice; do not disregard her), and let your treatment of her be very handsome." (*Dur-e-Mansoor, Baihaqi*)

Here we find the Prophet ﷺ advising that when parents call their son or daughter, he or she should respond at once and carry out whatever they have to say. This is in the normal course. Should you, however, be in your compulsory (*farz*) devotional prayers, and the situation at the moment is emergent, and the mother or father call you; for instance, he or she might have slipped and fallen down, or there is a strong possibility of a serious mishap, and there is no one to rush to help, the prayers should be discontinued at once. But if one has called in no such emergency, the prayers must not be interrupted.

If one is in the act of optional devotions (*navafil*) and the parent call you for some serious work or not, it will be counted a sin if you do not answer. But if they call you knowing that you are praying, it is not proper that you answer them or discontinue your devotions.

[*Shami, chapter: idrak-ul- Fariza*]

❖ ❖ ❖ ❖ ❖

Chapter : 3

PUNISHMENTS FOR DISOBEDIENCE TO PARENTS

DISOBEYING PARENTS IS ONE OF THE GREATER SINS

وعن عبد الله بن عمرو رضى الله تعالى عنهما قال: قال رسول الله صلى الله عليه وسلم: الكبائر الا شراك بالله وعقوق الوالدين وقتل النفس واليمين الغموس.

Abdullah bin Amr' reports the Prophet ﷺ said:. The great sins are:

i) *shirk*: ascribing partners to Allah, polytheism.

ii) uqooque: disobedience, and such of parents.

iii) homicide: (taking human life when not sanctioned by law)

iv) taking false oaths. (Bukhari incl. in *Mishkat-ul Masabih*)

These are the greatest of sins. The list of the lesser but still great sins is very long.

In the list quoted here, uqooque follows immediately after *shirk*. Uqooque has a wide sense; it includes troubling the parents in any way, offending them by word or action, disobedience, not spending on them when they need such help, and so on. What Allah loves most is prayers within the stipulated time and the best possible treatment of parents; similarly, of the great sins, offending the parents is listed immediately after *shirk*. How great a sin it is to disobey and offend parents is clear from this Tradition.

HUMILIATED IS HE WHOM HIS PARENTS HAVE NOT BROUGHT TO PARADISE

وعن ابی هریرة رضی الله تعالی عنه قال: قال رسول الله صلی الله علیه وسلم: رغم انفه رغم انفه رغم انفه۔ قیل: من یا رسول الله؟ قال: من ادرك والدیه عند الکبر احدهما او کلاهما ثم لم یدخل الجنة۔

Abu Hurairah tells us that on one occasion the Prophet ﷺ exclaimed (in a trance): "he is humbled, he is humbled, he is humbled"!

The Companions asked, "who is humbled, O Prophet ﷺ of Allah?"

The Prophet ﷺ answered, "he who found his parents or one of them in old age and did not enter paradise (by serving them)."(Muslim incl. in *Mishkat-ul-Masabih*)

We have already learnt that serving parents and treating them with magnanimity is the best way of entering paradise, and disobedience of parents and causing them pain is the way to be consigned to hell. During life, specially during youth, many great and small sins are committed and disobedience to parents also takes place. Therefore, should we see our parents live to old age, the opportunity should not be missed for making up for the past by serving them to the very best so as to do penance and save one's self from hell and become entitled to paradise. Should one even now persist in neglecting them, disobeying them and causing them offence after offence and not receive the blessings of his prayers, one only paves his way to certain perdition.

It is of such an one the Prophet ﷺ said that he is humiliated both in this world and the next. Therefore, one should always devotedly honour one's parents and , keeping them happy, earn the reward of paradise.

DOORS OF PARADISE ARE ALWAYS OPEN TO OBEDIENT CHILDREN, AND OF HELL TO THE DISOBEDIENT

وعن ابن عباس رضى الله تعالى عنهما قال: قال رسول الله صلى الله عليه وسلم: من اصبح مطيعا لله فى والديه اصبح له بابان مفتوحان من الجنة وان كان واحدا فواحد، ومن اصبح عاصيا لله فى والديه اصبح له بابان مفتوحان من النار ان كان واحدا فواحدا، قال رجل وان ظلماه، قال وان ظلماه وان ظلماه وان ظلما۔

From Ibn Abbas: The Prophet ﷺ said, "he who passes the night in the condition of obedience to Allah in respect of his parents has both the doors of paradise open to him; and if there be one parent, and the son passes the night in obedience to Allah in respect of him (or her), he has one door of paradise open to him in the morning; but if one passes the night in disobedience to Allah in respect of his parents he has both the doors of hell open to him, and if there be only one parent and the offspring passes the night in the condition of disobedience to Allah concerning his parent, he has one door of hell open to him in the morning."

Someone asked, "even if the parents tyrannised over him? "

Then the Prophet ﷺ exclaimed three times, "even if the parent tyrannised over him, even if the parent tyrannised over him!"

(Baihaqi incl. in *Mishkat-ul- Masabih*)

In this Tradition the importance of the blessings of filial devotion to parents and good treatment of them is fully brought out. And the curse of disobedience to them and offending their susceptibilities is also fully emphasised.

The words, "even though the parent tyrannise" do not imply that the parents are permitted to tyrannise. If they do so, they shall be answerable to Allah for their conduct, the punishment of which will fall on them. The duty of the offspring is to concern only about its own conduct, not of its parents.

This counsel is of vital importance for social collective life. Every individual should act according to his responsibilities, and not worry about what another does to him. How happy life would be if everyone, young or old, acted in the light of this counsel!

TO STARE AT PARENTS IS ALSO A DENIAL OF THEIR RIGHTS

وعن عائشة رضى الله تعالىٰ عنها قالت: قال رسول الله صلى الله عليه وسلم ما بَرَّ اَبَاهُ مَنْ حَدَّ اليه الطَّرْفَ، (كذا فى الدارالمنثور عن البيهقى فى شعب الايمان)

It is recorded on the authority of lady Ayesha that the Prophet ﷺ said; "he who gives his father a rude look has not dealt handsomely with him.

(*Dur-e-Mansoor Baihaqi in al-Sha'ab*)

This tradition tells us that even to stare at the parent or give him or her a harsh look is included in annoying them. Some one asked Imam Hasan what the limits of aqooque were, and he replied, "to deprive your parents of your service and your wealth; or discontinue seeing them; or give them a harsh look, is all a violation of their rights

(*Dur-e-Mansoor* from *Ibn Abi Sheba*)

Hazrat Arwah says; "If your parents do anything that angers you, anything you do not like, do not look at them with slanting eyes, This because hard looks are the first indication of anger."

(*Dur-e-Mansoor* from *Ibn Abi Hatim*)

This means that together with obedience and humility ingrained in the heart, one should also control one's looks and general behaviour so as to give no occasion whatever to slight a parent's sensitiveness.

TO ABUSE PARENTS IS THE GREATEST OF SINS

وعن عبدالله بن عمرو رضى الله تعالى عنه قال: قال رسول الله صلى الله عليه وسلم: من الكبائر شتم الرجل والديه، قالو: يا رسول الله وهل يشتم الرجل والديه قال: نعم يسب ابا الرجل فيسب اباه ويسب امه فيسب امه۔ (رواه البخاری ومسلم)

From Abdullah bin Amr: the Prophet ﷺ said: "among the greatest of sins is that one should abuse his own parents."

Someone asked, "O Prophet of Allah! is it possible that anyone should abuse his own parents?"

The Prophet ﷺ explained that one form of abuse was that a man should abuse another man's father and then this other man returns the abuse in the same words; or that he abuses another's mother, and the man returns the abuse in the same words.

(*Bukhari* and *Muslim* incl. *Mishkat*)

That is, though the abusing man has not abused his own father or mother, yet by virtue of his having abused another's parents, he has become the cause of having his own parents abused, and, therefore, he has virtually abused his own parents. Had he not abused the other person, he would not have had his own parents abused.

This the Prophet ﷺ declares, is among the greater sins. How much greater a sin would it then be directly to abuse one's own parents. According to the social norms prevailing in those times it appeared to the Companions as very surprising that one should abuse his own parents, and the Prophet Prophet ﷺ explained that this could be possible in such and such a case. But in our own times, we see that there are young men and women who use all manner of invectives for their parents and refer to them in unmentionable words and phrases.

ACCURSED IS HE WHO CURSES HIS PARENTS

وعن علی رضی الله تعالی عنه قال: ما خصنا رسول الله صلی الله علیه وسلم بشئی لم یخص به الناس الا ما فی قراب سیفی ثم اخرج صحیفة فاذا فیها مکتوب لعن الله من ذبح لغیر الله لعن الله من سرق منار الارض لعن الله من لعن والدیه لعن الله من اوی محدثا۔

Hazrat Ali tells us: "there is nothing the Prophet ﷺ particularised for us to the exclusion of other Muslims, except for what is in the scabbard of my sword."

He then pulled out a piece of parchment on which were written the words:

"Accursed be he who slaughters a beast in the name of any other than Allah; accursed be he who curses his father or mother; accursed be he who robs the markings on land; accursed be he who gives asylum to one who introduces innovations in Islam (by deed or theory)."

(*Al-Adab Al-Mufrad, Bukhari and Muṣlim, Kitab-ul-Adab*)

Here some people are mentioned as accursed:

1) Those who, instead of sacrificing for Allah's pleasure, for instance, during hajj, slaughter animals on a grave to please a pir or *faqeer*. This is *shirk* and an accursed deed.

2) Who intrude on the boundaries marked out on land (in Muslim the *ghayara*' is also mentioned). He who dishonestly alters the land -markings is also accursed. This is a crime that farmers and soil tillers frequently commit. Field boundaries are effaced to encroach on neighbouring plots. Similar misdeeds are committed on urban property as well, false maps and diagrams are drawn up; officials are bribed and forged entries made in registers. All this is accursed.

3) Those who curse their parents. The implication is clear. When even the exclamation *uff* is forbidden, how can abuse or invocation of a curse be permissible? Yet there are people, uneducated as well as cultured and educated, who do commit this gravest of sins. Another hadith Recorded in *Dur-e-Mansoor* from Hakim is: "Allah's curse is on him who troubles his parents."

4) Those who shelter an innovator in religion. Anything invented, introduced and foisted on religion is bid' at, innovation. Innovation may be theoretical or practical; both are unacceptable in Islam. To give shelter to an innovator is virtually to aid and abet the innovation and ,thus, to

reinforce it.

The words spoken to Ali, that the Prophet ﷺ did not particularise anything "for us" to the exclusion of other Muslims, except such and such, are reported by him according to his knowledge. The exceptions ; too; are not particularised for Ali, the Prophet ﷺ having merely intended to convey their importance and Ali, attaching the same importance to them, kept them well- guarded. The special safeguarding is the particularisation for Ali and his clan.

A sect believes that Ali was the Prophet's *wasi* (inheritor) by virtue of the testament or a will, and the Prophet ﷺ had told him some very special things. The Tradition quoted here negates any such belief. Had the Prophet ﷺ intended any thing to be kept in confidence, Ali would never have disclosed it. Besides, in the words, there is not a trace of any will or succession to the *khilafat*.

PERDITION FOR PARENTICIDE

وعن ابن عباس رضى الله تعالى عنهما قال: قال رسول الله صلى الله عليه وسلم ان اشد الناس عذابا يوم القيامة من قتل نبيا او قتله نبى او قتل احد والديه والمصورون وعالم لم ينتفع علمه.

It is on record from Ibn Abbas that the Prophet ﷺ said: " doubt not that on the Last Day the severest of punishment shall be for him who has slain a Prophet or is slain by a Prophet; and one who has killed his own mother or father; and he who draws a picture; and the learned man who does not profit by his learning."

(*Dur-e-Mansoor, Baihaqi;* Chapter on Pictures)

In this Tradition are mentioned those who merit the greatest of punishment, and included among them are those who kill their parents.

Quite possibly; in days gone by, it might have been unimaginable that anyone should be capable of deliberately doing one's own mother or father to death, but today to kill a parent over a land dispute or other matters, has become quite commonplace. Because Allah has commanded that the good treatment of parents is next only to serving Him, the murder of cither of them must be punishable with terrible severity.

HARASSING PARENTS IS PUNISHED IN THIS VERY LIFE

وعن ابى بكرة رضى الله تعالى عنه قال: قال رسول الله صلى الله صلى عليه وسلم: كل الذنوب يغفر الله منها ماشآء الا عقوق الوالدين، انه يعجل لصاحبه فى الحيوة قبل الممات۔

> We have from Abu Bakr that the Prophet ﷺ said: "Allah forgives all sins except the sin of offending parents, and offending them is a sin that He punishes in this very world."
>
> (*Baihaqi: Sha'b-al- Imaan*, incl. *Mishkat-al-Masabeeh*)

We have in one hadith that besides cruelty and discontinuance of good treatment of relatives, there is not a sin which deserves greater punishment. Moreover, the punishment of the hereafter is not replaced but is kept in store to be meted out later on.

(*Mishkat*)

That is, punishment for offending parents and not treating relatives well is awarded in both the worlds.

Today many a way is worked out to resolve serious problems

and overcome deficulties but those misdeeds are not abandoned on account of which troubles and anxieties come!

HE WHO OFFENDS HIS PARENTS WILL NOT ENTER PARADISE

وعن عبدالله عمرو رضى الله تعالى عنهما قال: قال رسول الله صلى الله عليه وسلم: لا يدخل الجنة منان ولا عاق ولا مدمن حمر.

Abdullah bin Amr has reported: the Prophet ﷺ said, "he who talks of having done a favour, and he who troubles his parents and he who takes intoxicants habitually shall not enter paradise."

(*Nisai, Darmi* incl. *Mishkat-al-Masabih*)

After giving someone anything or doing someone a good turn, and then to tell him how great a favour you have done him, negates the goodness of the deed. We have in the Qur'ãn:

يا ايها الذين آمنوا الا تبطلوا صدقاتكم بالمن والاذى.

" O you who believe! Do not destroy your charity by speaking of the favour or causing pain."

There are people who are in the habit of reminding those to whom they do a favour how great a good they have done them; a little good deed and mountains of obligational reminders! The obligated person is so bowed down under the weight and put to such great shame that he wishes he had never accepted the favour from such a mean, shallow person. The poor man does not profit by the favour as much as he loses by the pain caused to him.

In the hadith quoted here, we note that anyone who reminds another of a favour, and he who troubles his parents and one who is a habitual drunkard will not enter paradise; that is, such people will not be among the first to enter. If they die in Islam, they may enter paradise but only after they have undergone the punishment.

Whether relatives, friends or strangers, the act of reminding them of a favour is always bad and a great sin that prevents one from paradise.

We have already shown that punishment for troubling parents is given in both the worlds. Therefore, the guilty should make immediate amends, crave forgiveness of their parents and improve themselves in future by treating them with handsome behaviour.

In this *hadith*, the drunkard is also mentioned that he will not enter paradise. Such people too should reflect on the words and repent.

In another hadith we are told that everything that causes intoxication is forbidden. Allah will make an addict to intoxicants drink of طِينَةُ الْخَبَالِ [*Teenat-ul-Khabaal*].

The Companions asked. "O Prophet of Allah! what is *Teenat-ul-Khabaal*?"

The Prophet ﷺ explained, " the drained product of crushed, burning bodies in hell!"

Another hadith from Ahmad included in the *Mishkat-ul-Masabih* is: "My Lord the Glorious has promised that He will give one who drinks a mouthful of intoxicant, an equal amount of purified matter to drink; and he who gives up strong drink for fear of Him, will be given to drink from the holy pool of *Al-Kausar*.

Chapter : 4

WHAT SHOULD BE DONE IF THE PARENTS ARE NOT LIVING

وعن ابى اسيدن الساعدى رضى الله تعالىٰ عنه قال: بينا نحن عند رسول الله صلى الله تعالى عليه وسلم اذ جاء ه رجل من بنى سلمة۔ فقال: يا رسول الله هل بقي من برابوى شي ابرهما بعد موتهما قال: نعم، الصلوة عليهما والاستغفار لهما وانفاذ عهدهما من بعدهما وصلة الرحم التى لاتوصل الا بهما واكرام صديقهما۔

(رواه ابو داؤد، ابن ماجة كذا فى المشكوة)

> Abu Usayad reports:" we were present when a man of the Banu Salma came and asked the Prophet ﷺ, 'now that both my parents have passed away, is there anything that I yet may do to fulfil my obligations to them?'

The Prophet ﷺ answered, yes, you may invoke Allah's mercy on them: and you may pray that Allah may forgive their sins; and you may carry out any plan that they might have desired to implement; and you may continue to do for their pleasure the good works they used to do; and you may honour those they used to be familiar with."

(*Ibn Maja, Abu Dawood incl. Mishkat-al-Masabih*)

We learn that we ought to continue our duty to our parents in the best of manner even after they are no more on this earth. That is, such works as would profit them and delight them, should they get the news.

The Prophet ﷺ mentioned five things one ought to do in memory of one's parents:

- ❖ Pray for Allah's mercy for them,
- ❖ Invoke Allah's forgiveness of their sins; for instance, in the words:

رب اغفرلی ولوالدی

" O Lord! forgive me and forgive my parents."

* Implement the plan they wished to carry out.

The implications are broad. Specially, to execute their will which they might have made according to the Shariah for charitable purposes or for vicarious hajj or for giving to anyone not legal heir. This should be done without the least hesitation. The deceased had full right to dispose of one-third of his property as he pleased but only after deduction of his funeral expenses and any debt repayable by him.

A number of people do not fulfil the terms of their parent's will. They either misappropriate the whole or give a part of it to show that they have carried out the will in full. This is thoroughly wrong; to misappropriate willed property and put it to one's own use is forbidden. When the *shariah* apportions two-thirds for the heirs, to take possession of the remaining one-third is greed, an act of cruelty on one's own self as well as on the deceased. Even if the deceased had not made a will, the heirs should nevertheless distribute some of his assets by way of charity; but if a will has been left, it would be a gross violation of rights and negation of mercy and compassion if the execution of it is not made according to its terms.

The words إِنْفَاذُ عَهْدِهِمَا are found in the hadith. Besides disposal of property, other matters too may be included in the will. For instance, the will may required that such and such of the heirs should be taught to memorise the Qur'ãn and such another who may already have memorised the Qur'ãn, may be educated to become a scholar of religion; or that such and such daughter may be married to some particular devout man; and similar directions regrading matrimonial connections. Every detail must be executed with sincerity. In fact, even if the written will does not mention it but the heirs know that the deceased would have liked to do something in such and such manner, they should act upon it. Of course, nothing should be done that is against the *Shariah*.

Of the directions advised by the Prophet ﷺ, the fourth stipulation is:

وصلة الرحم التى لا توصل الابهما

That is, do such things out of compassion and regard as are related only to the parents and are for their pleasure. In other words, it should be understood that the basic relatives are mother and father, and whatever other relatives one has: brothers, sisters, uncles, aunts, cousins, however near or distant, are there solely because of the two parents. To deal handsomely with each one of them out of compassion, according to one's means and according to their grades of proximity, is a very laudable religious duty. One should be conscious of the fact that so and so is related in such and such way to the mother or father and treating him or her in a good manner will be very gratifying to the two of them. One may normally treat people well, but relatives of parents are specifically mentioned for special treatment.

The fifth counsel given is: اكرام صديقهما

That is honour the friends and acquaintances of the parents. This means continuing the acquaintance, and helping them monetarily according to means as well as by rendering them any service, within the shariah, they may be in need of. The conscious motive is important, that whatever you do is for the good pleasure of the parents and for continuing the acquaintance solely for their sake.

We have in one hadith:

ان من ابو البر: صلة الرجل اهل ودابيه بعدان يولى۔

" Of the good deeds one is to do good to your father, friends in his absence." (That is, when he may have passed away or be on a journey.)

After mentioning the good treatment of relatives , the Prophet ﷺ advised that those also should be treated well who used to know the parents with due affection. The Prophet ﷺ himself used to go so far that whenever a sheep was slaughtered in his house, he would send some pieces of mutton to the friends of lady Khadija long after she had passed away.

Because she had suffered in all manner of ways for him, he held her memory in the highest of esteem. If she was no longer there, her friends were the objects of his good treatment. This is an excellent example of fidelity and continuation of love such as would be a source of profound happiness to the soul of the deceased; that so long after, presents were still being given by her husband in her memory.

During a journey, Abdullah bin Umar came across a bedouin who was an acquaintance of his father. Recognising him, Abdullah gave him an ass to ride and also the turban he was wearing. Some of his fellow travellers told him that he need not have given away so much and no more than two *dirhams* would have been quite enough. Abdullah explained, "it is not the bedouin's status that I had to regard but that he is my father's friend. The Prophet ﷺ has said, 'keep the father's friendships in mind; do not discontinue them or your light will be put out.'

(*Bukhari, Al-Adab Al-Mufrad*)

PRAYING FOR PARENTS

وعن ابی هريرة رضی الله تعالی عنه قال: قال رسول الله صلی الله عليه وسلم: اذا مات الانسان انقطع عنه عمله، الامن ثلاثة الامن صدقة جارية او علم ينتفع به او ولد صالح يدعواله۔

> Abu Hurairah tells us that the Prophet ﷺ said: " when a man dies all his deeds come to an end but there are three deeds the benefits of which continues after him. One, *Sadqa-e-Jariyah* or lasting charity; two, knowledge which people continue to learn; and the virtuous children who pray for him. "
>
> (*Muslim*. Incl. *Mishkat-al Masabih*)

As long as a man lives the treasure of the reward of good deeds he does is piled up and stored for him for the Hereafter. When he dies the deeds come to an end and additions to the reward are also discontinued. But there are three things which are the result of his good deeds and of which the effects continue even after he dies and so the reward of them.

* First, jariyah charity. Jariyah charity is that of which the benefits are not ended with the act but continue after its performance, therefore, their reward,too, for the doer continues. For instance, the building of a mosque or religious educational institution or donating scholarships for good education, constructing water wells; in short any work of lasting public benefit. The man passes away having spent of his wealth, but the reward keeps increasing and his grades go on elevating higher and higher.

* Two, knowledge that benifits the public. The reward of this, too, continues after death. For instance, teaching the Qur'ãn and helping one to memorise it; or teaching prayers

or writing a book on religion or financing its publication; or helping one to become a *maulvi*. All this is jariyah charity. The maulvi will teach his acquired knowledge to his pupils, and they; in turn, will teach their pupils, and so on. He who is taught to pray will teach others to pray, and thus the chain of benefits continues generation after generation, each link is benifitted and benefits another, and so the reward, too, is apportioned to each while it is diminished for none.

* Three, the reward of the prayers virtuous children make for their parents is assigned to the parents. They go on benifiting a great deal if the prayers are made for their forgiveness and for the elevation of their grades. Prayers cost nothing to the children. Being the media of the children's birth and having brought them up, the parents have their deeds included in the prayers of their children, now grown up and able to pray. These prayers are looked upon as jariyah charity. If the parents by their labour make their children virtuous, the reward of the children's virtuous deeds is also assigned to the parents, nothing of the reward to the children being diminished.

Besides the children's prayer, the reward of anyone for another person is similarly apportioned. But the children are specifically mentioned because in their upbringing the parents' labour has so much to do. That is why their prayers are included in the deeds of the parents.

DISOBEDIENT CHILDREN WHO PRAY FOR THEIR PARENTS ARE WRITTEN DOWN AS OBEDIENT

وعن انس رضى الله تعالى عنه قال: قال رسول الله صلى الله عليه وسلم: ان العبد ليموت، والده او احدهما، وانه لعاق فلا يزال يدعوا لهما ويستغفر لهما حتى يكتبه الله بارا۔

Anas reports the Prophet ﷺ as saying: "sometimes it so happens that after the parents die, their child who had been disobedient during their life- time and used to harass them, now begins to pray for them and beseech forgiveness until Allah turns to him and accounts him as a doer of good to them."

(*Baihaqi.* incl. *Mishkat-al-Masabih*)

PRAYING FOR SALVATION OF PARENTS ELEVATES THEIR GRADES

وعن ابى هريرة رضى الله تعالى عنه قال: قال رسول الله صلى الله عليه وسلم ان الله عزوجل يرفع الدرجة للعبد الصالح فى الجنة، فيقول: يا رب انى لى هذه، فيقول: باستغفار ولدك لك۔

Abu Hurairah reports the Prophet ﷺ as saying, "there is no doubt that Allah the Great and Glorious elevates the station of His devotee in heaven. The man asks ' O Lord! whence is this elevation from? 'His Lord tells him,' it comes from the prayer your son has made for you."

(*Ahmad*)

We understand from these Traditions that to pray for our parents is a very great handsome treatment of them. It is one that can be kept up even after their death. At least, after the duty- prayers, one should offer a prayer for the parents; it costs nothing and they derive a lot of benefits.

To pray for the forgiveness of sins is a great blessing and beneficial act. Not only are sins forgiven, whatever shortcoming there is in the devotions is also compensated. Praying for parents, teachers, scholars and religious thinkers who have left this world are greatly beneficial for them.

This Tradition explains that Allah the Glorious elevates the status of a pious devotee in heaven and he asks in wonderment what this is due to. He is told that it is due to his offspring praying for him.

In another Tradition, the Prophet ﷺ tells us that there is no doubt that Allah the Great and Glorious sends down immense blessings on the residents of the graves, and the gift the living (on the earth) present to them is that they pray for their salvation. *(Baihaqi in Sha'b-Iman)*

One great benefit of praying for parents is that if the offspring has been offending them during their lives, his prayers for them have him accounted as a giver of good treatment, and as compensation for shortcomings in their devotions.

WARNING

One should visit the graves of one's parents, take a lesson from them, be reminded of death, meditate and recite some prayers. Women should not be allowed to visit graveyards, while the men should purge themselves of innovations and keep away from such activities as may directly or indirectly be suspected of ascribing associates with Allah.

There is also a Tradition to the effect that his sins will be forgiven who every Friday visits the graves or the grave of one of the parents and will be written down as one who treated his parents well.

(*Baihaqi* and *Abi- al- Dunya*)

And let it be remembered that visiting the graves is a repetitive act, and *isaal-e-sawab* or transmitting a reward by praying for 'rewarding' the dead is quite distinct. The two are not interdependent. The latter can be done even from a distance.

GIVING CHARITY ON BEHALF OF PARENTS

وعن ابن عباس رضى الله تعالى عنهما ان رجلا قال: قال يا رسول الله صلى الله عليه وسلم ان توفيت ولم توص افينفعها ان اتصدق عنها قال نعم۔

> Ibn Abbas narrates: " A man came to the Prophet ﷺ and said, 'my mother has passed away. If I give any charity on her behalf, will it be of benefit to her?'
>
> 'Yes it will benefit her, the Prophet ﷺ confirmed."
>
> (*Bukhari*)

In another Tradition we are told that S'ad bin Ibada asked the Prophet ﷺ, my mother is no more, and I want to know what charity will be best on her behalf."

The Prophet ﷺ advised, " the charity of water."

Sa'd then had a water–well constructed and dedicating it said, "this is for Sad's mother"!

Lady 'A'isha tells us that a man came to the Prophet ﷺ saying that his mother died unexpectedly and that if she had the time to speak she would have said that she wanted to give charity. Now, if he donated in charity on her behalf whether she would get the reward for it. The Prophet ﷺ replied that she would (*Bukhari, Muslim*)

We learn from these Traditions that we should continue *Isaal-e-Sawab*, doing things for crediting Divine reward to parents by giving of charity in their behalf. The Tradition regarding S'ad bin Ibada indicates that making provision for water supply is a superior charity because water is a necessity of all living creatures fulfilling all manner of mundane and religious requirements. S'ad had a water–well constructed and dedicated it permanently as a continuous us charity, *Sadqa-e-Jariyah*, became the medium of a great reward.

In days gone by, a water-well had great importance. Even today it is a great necessity in the jungles, villages and smaller towns, while running water pipes are used in the cities. Therefore, if anyone has water tank built, or water-pipes laid or contributes to the payment of water consumption bills, his deed would be counted as a great charity and bring immense reward to him. Mosques and schools in the cities even today require wells as the government pipes some times run dry and there is a shortage of water. Hand water- pumps provided to schools, mosques and in various public places would be notable contributions.

WARNING

If the parents die leaving an uncleared debt and they have left provision for it, it is a bounden duty that the debt be repaid even though the heirs have nothing left for themselves and whether a will was made or not. If a will was made, the duty will be all the more pressing. If the deceased leave nothing behind, the heirs should dear the debt in any case. This would be a magnificent act on their part, one that would rescue the parents from a grave accountability on the Last Day. The act of repayment of debt is superior to giving in charity on their behalf.

Imam Auzai reports a Tradition that he who harasses his parents, but clears their debt, prays for their salvation, abuses no one on their behalf, is written down as one who treated them well; while he who may have treated his parents well during their lives, but does not clear the debt due from them, nor prays for their salvation and abuses people on them, nor prays for their salvation and abuses people on their behalf, will be written down as having maltreated them. (*Dur-e-Mansoor*)

PERFORMING HAJJ OR UMRAH ON BEHALF OF PARENTS

وعن ابى رزين العقيلى رضى الله تعالى عنه اتى النبى صلى الله عليه وسلم فقال: يا رسول الله ان ابى شيخ كبير لا يستطيع الحج ولا العمرة ولا الظعن قال: حج عن ابيك واعتمر.

Hazrat Abu Razeen bin Uqail tells us that he presented himself before the Prophet ﷺ, and asked him whether he could perform the great pilgrimage, hajj; or *umrah*, the lesser, on behalf of his father who was very old and too weak to perform either; and the Prophet ﷺ said, "you can do both on your father's behalf."

(*Tirmidhi, Abu Dawood, Nisai Incl Mishkat-al Masabih*)

وعن ابن عباس رضى الله تعالىٰ عنهما قال: ان امراة من خثعم قالت: يا رسول الله ان فريضة الله على عبادة فى الحج، ادركت ابى شيخا كبيرا، لايثبت على الراحلة افا حج عنه قال: نعم وذلك فى حجة الوداع.

Ibn Abbas reports that a woman of the Banu Khasham asked the Prophet ﷺ on the occasion of the Farewell Pilgrimage if she could perform hajj on behalf of her father who was very old and unable to ride his mount properly, and he replied, "yes, you can perform hajj on his behalf."

(*Bukhari, Muslim. Incl. Mishkat-al-Masabih*)

The two Traditions apprise us of the importance and blessing of vicarious hajj, and also that like hajj; *umrah*, too, can be thus performed.

The last mentioned Tradition also clarifies that a woman can perform hajj on behalf of an infirm man. Therefore, a man can perform hajj on behalf of a woman. Besides, it is not necessary that the person on whose behalf hajj or umrah is performed should be deceased. It can be performed on behalf of the living also. However, it is necessary that at the time of donning the pilgrimage robes, *ahram*, the motive should be that this is being done on behalf of such and such person. The rest of the rituals are the same as for one performing the pilgrimage on one's own.

It should be easy for people who travel frequently through Hijaz or who live there permanently to perform a pilgrimage on behalf of another, after they have performed one for themselves; indeed, to perform hajj and *umrah* repeatedly. To perform either pilgrimage on another's behalf it is not necessary to appoint a *wakil*, nor to take anyone's permission or inform anyone. However, if the disabled person be alive, it would be better to inform him so that he may be happy and pray for the pilgrim.

If hajj was due on a parent but the parent did not perform it for any reason whatever, and stipulated in his will that after his death someone should perform it on his behalf, the expenses being met out of the assets left by him, it will be an incumbent duty on the heirs to have the hajj performed accordingly. But this will be done only after any debt left by the deceaded has been repaid and the funeral expenses met from one-third of the assets. The remaining two-third will be distributed among the heirs. Should one third of the assets be not sufficient it would be an act of great virtue if the heirs make up the balance from their own share. If, however, the heirs refuse to do so, they may arrange for the performance of the vicarious hajj out of the one-third by someone nearer to Makkah. On principle, it is only one-third of the deceased's assets that can be willed whether for charitable purpose, distribution among the non- heirs, or any other.

The heirs or the executers of the will are duty bound to dispose off the one-third exactly according to the terms of it. If they do not so comply, misappropriate whole or part of it or spend it against these terms, their action will be *haram* (illicit), and haram also their consuming of it, of which they will be held grossly sinful.

Some people hold back all their parents ' assets and quite against their will do not have the vicarious hajj performed, while some give one or two-hundred *Riyals* to a pilgrim- guide, *muallim*, only to deceive themselves that they have carried out their duty and had the vicarious hajj performed. This is a violation of the will , its terms are not fulfilled and the doubt remains that no one might have performed the hajj as arranged. Experienced pilgrims testify that the muallim never helps a pilgrim for a couple of hundred *Riyals*. At best , the moneys given by various people for a number of vicarious hajj are collected and one person is made to go through the ceremonies and instructed to pray for all on whose behalf the collection was made. In this manner no one's hajj is performed. This should be clearly understood, a vicarios hajj must begin from the town or village where the deceased lived. That is, the pilgrimage must begin from the place where the deceased would have donned the pilgrim's robe and travelled by the route, had he lived.

When the law prescribes two-thirds for the heirs on such condition that not a jot more than one third can be enforced (unless the heirs permit), justice demands that if not out of their own share, at least, one-third from the assets of the owner be disposed off according as he desired in his will. Even if the deceased had not made out a will and had not performed a hajj, his children should, of their own accord, perform a hajj on his behalf or send someone else to do so, after, of course. Performing their own hajj. This would be an act of tremendous goodness towards the parents, and, it is hoped that Allah would accept their hajj. If the hajj was not due on the parents but later the children make enough money, they should, after performing their own hajj, have one performed on the deceased's behalf. This would be the best of *silah-e-rahmi*. The life of this world is but short, and wealth, too, comes and goes; therefore, every opportunity should be availed of. To be miserly in matters of the Hereafter is very foolish, indeed. One Tradition tells us that Allah, the Great and Glorious, takes three people to paradise in return for one vicarious hajj : he on whose behalf the hajj is performed ; he who performs the hajj on behalf of the deceased and he who enables another to perform the hajj, whether out of his own wealth or according to the terms of the deceaded's will.

We have in one Tradition that he who performs hajj on behalf of his parents after they have passed away is protected against the fire of hell. The reward of the parents is that of a full hajj and the reward of the performer is not diminished. And there is no greater good deed for a relative should anyone perform a hajj on behalf of another and pray for its reward to be given to who lies in his grave.

In another Tradition we are told that the reward of him who performs a hajj on another's behalf is the same as that of the one on whose behalf the hajj is performed.

(All Traditions from *Kanz-ul-A'maal*)

Chapter : 5

DOING GOOD TO RELATIVES OTHER THAN PARENTS

وعن ابى هريرة رضى الله تعالى عنه قال: قال رسول صلى الله عليه وسلم: تعلموا من انسا بكم ماتصلون به ارحامكم، فان صلة الرحم محبة فى الاهل مثرآة فى المال منساة فى الأ ثر۔

> Abu Hurairah reports that the Prophet ﷺ said: "find your relatives out, trace their ancestries so that you may do good to them, because doing good to them will establish love among you and will increase your wealth and also your life-span."
>
> (*Tirmidhi. incl. Mishkat-al-Masabih*)

This hadith commands, first, that we make a search for our relatives and trace the ancestries of our parents; that is, try to find out how far the family branches spread and who, far or near, is related to us and in what way .Then, we are told that doing good to relatives is held very high in Islam; and good must be done to them according to means and nearness of relationship. That is why it is necessary to ascertain who is what to us. Three benefits of doing them good are mentioned.

First, that mutual love is established. When we visit one another, sympathise with them in their distress, assist them with money or service, it is obvious that they will love us in return. If all the individuals of the family do good to one another, hearts would become one of peace and happiness.

Second; that wealth increases by being good and nice to relatives.

Third, the life-score increases.

Both these results have been mentioned earlier in the paragraphs on " doing good to parents."

Good deeds to relatives please Allah (if the good is done with Islamic motives). When one does so many things to increase his wealth, he might as well experiment with this method also. Allah does not promise of wealth by other means, but He does promise increase if handsome treatment is extended to relatives.

Besides, such treatment is also a prescription for increasing the life-score. This, too, is included in Allah's promise.

Everyone is familiar with the fact that good deeds will bring good and evil deeds will bring evil in the Hereafter. But many are quite ignorant of the fact or do not give it sufficient importance, that in this very life good deeds bring many benefits and keep away a lot of sufferings that result from evil deeds. They go in pursuit of worldly methods and since they also engage themselves in evil, their endeavours end in failure. Not only do existing pain and sufferings continue, other afflictions keep popping up.

It has already been mentioned in a previous Tradition that the evil consequences of harassing parents and not doing good to relatives confront one in this very life and the punishment in the life Hereafter is besides. Just as causing parents to suffer and not doing good to other relatives is the cause of suffering in this life and the next, so is treating them well is the means of increasing wealth and life. The peculiar characteristics that Allah has given to every particular deed must show up whether or not one is acceptable to Him, or one may or may not be awarded the reward of his actions in the Hereafter. Abdullah bin Abbas quotes the Prophet ﷺ as saying, "when the members of a family treat one another well, Allah appoints providence for them and they remain in the protection of the Lord, the Merciful One."

And Abdul Rehman bin Auf quotes: "the act of obedience Allah rewards very soon is that of doing good to relatives; and the influence of this goodness is such that even though the members of the family may be evil doers yet their wealth increases and their numbers grow."

And he also said, "what brings perdition fastest is tyranny and false oaths."

Then he added, "false oaths devour wealth and finish it, render mercy unproductive, and ruin habitated towns. (*Dur-e-Mansoor*)

Abu Hurairah reports the Prophet ﷺ as having declared:

> "When spoils of war are made personal property (that is, the rich and the office holders take possession of them and do not allot to the poor their rightful share);
>
> people look upon trusts as war spoils (that is as personal property of the trustee for his own use), and upon Zakat as a penalty;
>
> acquire (religious) knowledge on behalf of another, husbands take orders from their wives;
>
> transfer obedience from their mothers to their wives and disobey the mother;
>
> seek nearness to friends and distance from the father;
>
> speak loudly in places of worship;
>
> the evil doer becomes leader of his tribe;

> State responsibility comes to rest with the meanest of the people;
>
> a man is honoured because of the fear of him;
>
> singing women and music instruments become openly immodest;
>
> intoxicants are consumed profusely;
>
> and people invoke curses on preceding generations, then await the time of red storms, earthquakes, sinking of the earth, faces becoming distorted and stones raining from the skies; and await signs that begin to appear like the breaking of a string and its beads falling from the skies; and await signs that begin to appear like the breaking of a string and its beads falling on one another in rapid succession."
>
> (*Tirmidhi*)

In this Tradition, it will have been noted, mentioned among the signs that portend evil are that husbands will take orders from their wives, there will be disobedience of the mother and preferential treatment of friends in place of the father.

Together with other great sins, it is becoming common that husbands are becoming so slavish to their wives that they no longer look upon their mothers as occupying any place of respect; they themselves harass the mother and also happily tolerate however the wife may rudely speak to her, or cause her any suffering or pain. Similarly, they treat their friends most lavishly, but far from rendering any service to the father look upon his very existence as a nuisance, They spend a great deal of time among friends but find none for their father, nor take him seriously nor serve him in any way. Some of them are so foolish that they treat their parents as servants and like mighty lords order them about.

Among the signs of the coming of the Last Day is that women will give birth to children who will rule over them. (*Muslim*)

This prophecy is already taking shape before our eyes. Is it surprising that calamities should come when such are the social conditions today?

Allah is Guide absolute!

وعن ابی رمثة رضی الله تعالی عنه قال: انتهیت الی رسول الله صلی الله علیه وسلم فسمعته یقول: برامك وا باك و اختك واخاك ثم ادناك و ادناك۔

> Abu Rimtha reports that one day when he appeared before the Prophet ﷺ, he found him telling someone, " treat your mother and your father and your sister and your brother well, and after them, treat your other relatives well in order of their nearness to you."

In this Tradition , sisters and brothers are also mentioned along with one's mother and father. Then, "those near to you in order of nearness" All of them must be treated handsomely.

The idea is that since all the relatives are not equally related, some are distant, some near, and even among the near, some are nearer , and among the distant, some are more distant, some less, the principle laid down is that of comparative proximity, the nearer having the greater right on us. This principle concerns financial help and personal service, otherwise all are to be equally treated. Permanent severance of acquaintance with any fellow Muslim is entirely forbidden. How then can it be permissible for relatives ?

In exceptional cases of dire need, however, the comparative proximity principle is to be waived, urgent cases deserving our immediate attention.

(Relevant details are given in the various books on *fiqah* and, if necessary, information may be obtained from the *ulama*).

There are people who actually tyrannise over brothers and sisters. This Tradition applies to them particularly. Brother-sister relationship is because of the common parentage ,and should be specially respected; handsome treatments of them and doing them good should be their special concern. But what we see today is that sometimes the elder brother and sister bully and persecute the younger, or the younger brother or sister commit excesses on the elder. Instead of spending on them they deprive them of their rightful share. Whatever they receive of an inheritance is wholly misappropriated. Without dividing it according to law, the whole is spent on one's own wife and children while the brothers and sisters, after being looked after, at the most, for three or four years, are deprived of their rightful property. By the time ones grow up they find that nothing is left for them and the property is transferred to the usurper's children. Such cases come to light quite frequently; and if the deceased leaves behind two wives, the inheritance is hardly ever divided among them. Whatever is already in the possession of the children of one wife is guarded jealously. Everyone wants to take from the other but does not prepare one's spirit to give to the other. This is a very great violation of the principle of handsome treatment of relatives. Some families hardly ever allow the sister any share in the parents's legacy, and on the excuse that the sisters have voluntarily waived their right; devour all their share. Even the self-righteous who issue honesty certificates do not lag behind in this.

Some brothers request their sisters to waive their right in the inheritance in favour of them, and the girls thinking it would be unwise to spoil relations with the brothers as, in any case, it will be impossible to get anything from them, and, having no alternative; reluctantly concede the request. Such waiver is illegal in *shariah*, It would be different if the girl's share were transferred to her name, and if she were given possession of it and, thereafter, she gave it voluntarily to her brother or brothers.

The words in the Tradition to the effect that after mother and father, sister and brother the relatives should be treated well according to the nearness of relationship, also mean that the nearer the relationship the better the treatment should be. Good treatment does not merely imply financial help but also giving presents, serving in various ways, visiting, sharing of joys sorrows, and needs, and keeping up correspondence, if far away. All this is included in "handsome treatment" In most of these things there is no financial expenditure involved, only pleasantness and affection. Therefore, do as much good as possible.

RESPECT FOR MOTHER'S SISTER

وعن ابن عمر رضى الله تعالى عنهما ان رجلا اتى النبى صلى الله عليه وسلم فقال: يارسول الله انى اصبت ذنبا عظيما فهل لى من تو بة فقال: هل لك من ام قال: لا قال: وهل لك من خالة قال: نعم قال: فبرها

Ibn Umar reports that a man came to the Prophet ﷺ and said, " I have committed a very great sin and I wonder if it can be forgiven." The Prophet ﷺ asked, " have you a mother?"

The man answered that he had lost his mother.
" Then , is her sister alive?"
"She is", the man said.

'Then go and treat her well, "the Prophet ﷺ advised him. (Tirmidhi, Inc,. in *Mishkat-al-Masabih*)

This Tradition commands good treatment of the maternal aunt. In another Tradition we have the words الخالة بمنز لة الام "a maternal aunt is on the same level as mother." (*Bukhari*)

She looks upon her sister's children as her own and cherishes a mother's kindness towards them. In the opinion of the *fuqaha* (jurists), if the mother dies, the first right to the bringing up of her children is that of her sisters, even in preference to their grandmother or sister, the reason being her emotions of kindness. Even during the mother's life, the maternal aunt should be frequently visited and treated well. More so after the mothers, death because she now occupies the mother's position.

The Prophet ﷺ commands that the penance (*kuffara*) for a great sin is service and good treatment of the maternal aunt in lieu of the mother when the mother is no more , and thus have Allah forgive the sins. Besides the maternal aunt, the other relatives connected through the mother should also be handsomely treated; the grandmother and grandfather, their children, and children's children; maternal uncle, all have right to our service and handsome treatment.

RESPECT FOR FOSTER MOTHER

وعن ابى الطفيل رضى الله تعالى عنه قال: رأيت النبى صلى الله عليه وسلم يقسم لحماء بالجعرانة اذا اقبلت امرأة حتى اذنت الى النبى صلى الله عليه وسلم، فبسط لها رداءه، فجلست عليه، فقلت: من هى؟ فقالوا: هي امه التى ارضعته.

> Abu Tufail reports: "I saw the Prophet ﷺ distributing meat in Jarrana when a woman came and made her way to the place where he was; and he spread his cloak-sheet for her to sit on .Seeing this I asked those near me who she might be and they told me that she was his foster mother who had nursed him when he was an infant."
>
> (*Abu Dawood*, Incl. *Mishkat-al -Masabih*)

This Tradition shows the importance of honouring and doing good to women who nurse us when we are very small.

Commentaries of this Tradition inform us that the lady who visited the Prophet ﷺ on this occasion was Halima Sa'dia who had taken the infant Prophet to be from Makkah to her clan; the Banu Sa'd, nursed him and brought him up for the first few years.

Whether she ever accepted Islam or not is questionable but immaterial to us. What is important is that every respect is due to a woman related to us by breast- feeding. Such relation is equivalent to that of a mother's, and all laws of haram (forbidden) are similarly applicable. Therefore, the foster-mother, her husband and children and other relatives also merit our respect and good treatment of them.

EVIL CONSEQUENCES OF DISCONTINUING GOOD

وعن عبد الله بن ابی اوفی رضی الله تعالی عنه قال: سمعت رسول الله صلی الله علیه وسلم یقول: ماتنزل الرحمة علی قوم فیهم قاطع رحم۔

> Abdullah bin Abi Aufi tells us that he heard the Prophet ﷺ say: "blessings do not come down on a people among whom there is one person who discontinues doing good to relatives."
>
> (Baihaqi, Incl. Mishkat-al Masabih)

Just as Allah sends down His blessings on people dedicated to handsome treatment of one another, so also does He hold back His blessings on those who back out of such treatment. And not only on those individuals who discontinue this goodness but on all those to whose community he belongs, the reason being that when one man discontinues the goodness , others do not urge him to continue and, instead, themselves begin to follow his example.

وعن ابی هریرة رضی الله تعالی عنه قال: قال رسول الله صلی الله علیه وسلم : الرحم شجنة من الرحمن فقال: الله من وصلك وصلته ومن قطعك قطعته۔

> Abu Hurayra reports the holy Prophet ﷺ as saying, "the word rahm is affiliated to the word Rahman, which

is the name of Allah the Glorious, and Allah the Glorious says, 'you who have kept united to rahm, I shall keep you united (by My mercy) to Myself but you who disconnect yourselves from rahm, I shall disconnect from My mercy."

(*Bukhari. Incl. Mishkat-al- Masabih*)

We have in one Tradition: لا يدخل الجنة قاطع الرحم۔

"He who discontinue good deeds to relatives shall not enter paradise."

This means that the punishment for this sin is given in this life as well as in the Hereafter. In some families year after year passes and mutual relations are not normalised. Even blood is shed while litigation has become the customary routine. Brother stands pitched against brother; uncle against nephew; brother against sister. Some have taken wrongful possession of residential property; another of rural land ,killing and being killed goes on; there is no wishing salutations;if they come across another each turns his face away. This has no place in Islam. If life were conducted on the principles of silah-e-rahmi ..... mutual doing good among relatives.....in-fighting would cease. But these principles are not followed and future generations have to suffer the consequences.

RETURNING GOOD FOR GOOD IS NOT SILAH-E-RAHMI

وعن ابن عمر رضى الله تعالى عنه قال: قال رسول الله صلى الله عليه وسلم ليس الواصل بالمكافئ ولكن الواصل الذى اذا قطعت رحمه وصلها۔

Ibn Umar reports the Prophet ﷺ as saying , " he who merely returns a good deed for a good deed is not a doer of *silah-e-rahmi*. A doer of silah-e-rahme is one to whom good is not done, nevertheless, he does good to relatives."

This Tradition advises those people who argue that since none of their relatives does any good to them, why should they bother to go out of their way and do good to him. They complain that an uncle has done such and such or a nephew so and so, therefore......? The Prophet ﷺ says, " if your brother and sister, and aunt and uncle meet you very nicely ; you also treat them well in return and think that you have fulfilled your obligation of *Silah-e-Rahmi*; but this is not *Silah-e-Rahmi* which the *shariah* requires, because this is doing no more than paying back. *Silah-e-Rahmi* is to do good even when the other does no good to you. Continue meeting those who do no good to you, and now and then give them a present. This will entail some exertion of will -power but the reward, *Inshaallah*, is bound to be great. And he who has,not been doing good to you will very likely abandon his way and emulate you. If every member of the family acted on this principle, the whole family would become an embodiment of mercy for all.

Aqba bin Aamir reports, "I met the Prophet ﷺ and quickly grasped his hand and he grasped mine. Then he said, "Uqba, shall I not tell you of the virtues of the people of this world and the next?' and continued , 'do not break off relations with one even if one breaks off relations with you and give him who deprives you and forgive him who commits an excess against you. "Then he said, "and be warned that he who wants that his life-span increase and his livelihood, he should do good by his relatives." (*Hakim*)

CONCLUSION

This is in two sections : the first, regarding education of children in religion and good manners; the second, on the implementation of the rights of parents. In respect of the first, it will be enough to qoute the relevant Tradition with due commentary.

EDUCATION AND DISCIPLINE OF CHILDREN

وعن معاذ رضى الله تعالى عنه قال: اوصانى رسول الله صلى الله عليه وسلم بعشر كلمات قال: لا تشرك بالله وان قتلت وحرقت ولا تعقن والديك ، وان امراك ان تخرج من اهل ومالك ولا تتركن صلوة مكتوبة متعمدا، فان من ترك صلوة متعمدا فقد برئت منه ذمة الله ولاتشربن خمرا، فانه رأس كل فاحشة، واياك والمعصية، فان بالمعصية حل سخط الله، واياك والفرار من الزحف وان هلك الناس، واذا اصاب الناس موت، وانت فيهم فاثبت وانفق على عيالك من طولك، ولا ترفع عنهم عصاك ادبا واخفهم فى الله۔

Mu'a"az relates: "the Prophet ﷺ advised me ten things:

a. do not ascribe partners to Allah even if you should be killed or burnt alive;

b. do not trouble your parents, even though they order you to renounce your family and wealth;

c. do not wilfully give up your duty- prayers, because Allah ceases to be responsible for him who does so;

d. never take to alcoholic drinks, because it is the root of all shamelessness;

e. avoid sin, because sin brings the wrath of Allah on one,

f. do not run away from a field of battle, though all others may be slain;

g. when there is an epidemic of plague and you are there, do not go away but stay there;

h. spend the best part of your wealth on your family;

i. ever keep your rod ready to discipline your children and never lay it by;

j. and keep them aware of the obedience and fear of Allah.

The ten counsels given in this Traditon are very significant. Sizeable commentary may be written on each one of them , but here we shall deal only summarily with them, attaching special importance to b, h, i, and j.

a. The first counsel is that there shoud be no shyrk , ascribing of partners to the Divine being or assigning His attributes to someone else, in theory or by practical deeds. Should an individual or any group compel us to shyrk such belief must not be accepted, even if it means being killed or being set on fire.

Although it is permissible , for the sake of saving life, to utter a verbal denial (*kufr*), it is infinitely better to die than utter a word against the true faith.

b. The second counsel is that we are never to trouble our parents in any way whatever , even if they order us out of the house. This indicates the importance of obedience to them. However , it is only a hypothetical condition. No sensible or loving parent will ever give such an order. Obedience is not binding if words to that effect are sounded out of anger or ignorance. The parents are not permitted to give such an order, but the children are directed to have their ego so disciplined that even if they are so ordered, they should be ready to obey.

c. The third counsel is that the duty- prayers must never be wilfully given up; and the warning is emphasised that wilful renunciation of prayers means that Allah will then not help one in this life nor in the Hereafter nor give one any security or peace.

d. The foruth is regarding abstinence from drinking, which by itself is a great sin. and also leads to every other sin. The drunk does not remain in his senses and does whatever occurs to him. In another tradition strong drink is described as "the key to every mischief." It is also called "mother of foolish words and deeds."People who have seen addicts of strong drink will vouch that all this is correct.

e. Fifth counsel: commit no sin, because sin invites Allah's displeasure, accounting is demanded and this means punishment. The traditions detail the kind of evil results that follow different evil deeds, and the different blessings that come from different good deeds.

f. Sixth counsel: do not flee battlefield even when you see all your fellows-in arms get killed. Running away from a battle is a great sin, from which may Allah preserve Muslim! These days, alas! Muslims have given up *jihad* in the path of Allah and are, therefore, deprived of its blessings.

g. Seventh counsel : that when there is an epidemic of plague in any place, those already there must not go away but stay there, but those away from the place, (as advised in another tradition) should not go there. (*Bukhari, Muslim*)

This counsel is based on several sound reasons : the people not infected by the epidemic should stay back to look after the victims and bury those who die, otherwise the dead bodies would just lie around exposed and undisposed of. We should trust Allah and know that if death is to come it will come any where.

Lady 'A'isha has reported the Prophet ﷺ as advising that a person is presented the reward of a martyr if being already in a place infected by an epidemic, patiently remains there with a virtuous motive and trusting no suffering can come to him save one that Allah wills.

And one more good reason for advising people not to go-to an epidemic infected area is that if they go there and get infected, they might think that if they had not come they would not have had to suffer in this way. Such thinking would be a weakness of faith in Allah. There are other reasons too.

h. Eighth conusel: spend of your best on your family.

i. Ninth counsel: continue educating and discipling them; do not relent, do not spare the rod.

j. And last; keep the family conscious of the fear of Allah.

Of these counsels, three are connected with the upbrining of the children and looking after the family. The idea is that there should be no stingering on expenditure on the family's welfare; we must not deprive them of Allah's blessings lest they begin to look elsewhere for them. Together with their physical requirements their religion should not be neglected. That is, they should be educated in good manners, and what the commands of Allah are, how they must be acted upon, and how life should be lived in the midst of fellow-creatures.

Not sparing the rod only implies that there should be no relenting in carrying out these objectives and the family should not be given occasion to think that parents are not much interested in the religious upbringing of their offspring. To establish them on the path of religion and make them faithful the parent must be stern and strict; their progress and what they do should be kept under constant vigilance and if they have to be rebuked, they should be rebuked, and even thrashed, if need be.

This does not mean that beating up is the only way to bring up a child or that the child should be beaten day and night, but that he should not be allowed to feel any weakening in the parents's attitude. He must understand that he should be alert all the time, otherwise he will be physically punished. At the same time tact and method and verbal guidance should be used wisely . Make him understand that this world is mortal, and the Hereafter immortal. And teach him that Allah is the Creator and Owner, to know Him is essential; obedience to Him gives good shape to life in this world and the next; He is Compassionate and Merciful and also Severe in punishment. We must have hope in Him and also fear Him; and remember in how many ways His mercy keeps us in His blessings. Explain all this to the child and also make him realise that Allah's grasp is quick and tight. If the children are brought up in this way, they will, in-sha Allah , become truly religious ; they will hold the Prophet ﷺ as very dear to their hearts, will live up to his counsels and also be ever at the service of their parents. Experience shows that whenever anyone indifferent to his parents comes into the company of religious people and begins to learn the lesson of the Hereafter, one also becomes conscious of the rights of his parents and his obligations to them.

Today people generally look upon the religious upbringing of their children as unhealthy and bad. From the very beginning they mould them in the ways and attire of the unbelievers. Instead of teaching them the Qur'ãn and hadith and Islamic commands, manners and mannerisms, they give them a different education, fearing lest they become mullahs! Since they are kept away from religion and religious people, by the time they grow up to the age of discretion, they neither know Allah nor the Prophet ﷺ, nor do they have any regard for their parents. In the eyes of these fashion devotees, the status of the parent is even less than that of an aged household servent. Basically the fault is that of the parents who placed them on the path of wrong and kept them ignorant of Islam. Now why should there be any complaint if the children treat them badly?

If a parent dies, the son comes laughing and giggling on the occasion to the funeral prayers but does not participate in them. The imam of the locality leads the prayers and if the son does line up, he knows nothing about the prayers.

The children are to blame that even after growing up they made no effort to get acquainted with the shariah, but the deceased whose coffin lies in front there, is also to be blamed, because he was the head of the family and educated his offspring in secularism, the ways and models of the unbelievers, but deprived them of the education of Islamic requirements.

Children who are oblivious of the demands of religion are also ignorant of parental rights. They neither revere nor pay any regard to their parents, nor pray for their salvation after the parents die; nor give any charity on their behalf, nor invoke blessings for them.

Parents who destory the religious life of their children should expect nothing from them in this life nor, after death, await their prayers and offerings. Why should he pray and give charity who has not been taught the importance of prayer, charity and Divine forgiveness?

فاعتبروا يا اولى الابصار

The following paragraphs are abbreviated from the last chapter of Ashraf Ali Thanvi's *Bahishti Gauhar*.

Ashraf Ali Thanvi gives us the reason for writing this chapter, namely, that just as there are people who overlook the Qur'ãnic verses and Traditions concerning the rights of parents, and so take the curse of such negligence on themselves, there are others who exaggerate on behalf of parental rights. That is, they go beyond the proper limits in their obedience to parents, thereby depriving the wife and children of their rights. Not asserting the latter, those categorical injunctions are overlooked which command their rights and thus the curse of the violation of these rights comes to lie squarely on their heads.

There are yet others who do not deprive anyone of his rights, but take the non-dutiful rights as dutiful. Sometimes this strains their capacity and they begin to think that the demands of the shariah are too severe and unbearable. This leads to depriving the rightful ones of their legitimate rights. Therefore, it is necessary to distinguish between the essential as duty and the non-essential and extra-duty.

The author then quotes from the Traditions, Fiqh and commentaries and, finally, gives his own conculsions briefly:

* If parents demand disobedience to what is commanded by the shariah, their demand must not be carried out.
* It is not premissible to spend on the parents if circumstances

are such that spending on them would deprive the wife and children of their lawful rights.

* If the wife tells her husband that she cannot live together with his parents and, therefore, he must provide for her seprately, it is binding on him to do so. If his parents demand that she must live together, their demand is not binding on him.

* Obedience to parents is not permitted if they demand doing what is impermissible in shariah, for instance, engaging in service where it is forbiddeen, or observing pagan practices, or shaving the beard.

Where an option is left to the individual, that is, where the *shariah* neither commands nor forbids, the subject should be decided on its merits. Suffering should not be unnecessary. For instance, if the circumstances are very bad and one wants to travel out in search of a livelihood but the parents tell him not to go, obedience to them is not necessary. But if the circumstances are not pressing enough the hazards of the journey should be taken into account and it should also be considered whether there are servants and others or not to look after the parents; and so on.

a. Disobedience is not permitted if there is danger on the way or there is likelihood of the parents suffering greatly. For instance, if he is going to fight in a war not commanded by the shariah,or if he is going overseas but he cannot provide for their comfort, and the work itself is not essentail and the journey; too is unnecessary.

b. But if there is no such reason for staying back, the journey is quite permissible, the parents' objections notwithstanding, but it is better that he stays back with them.

c. Obedience to parents is not permitted it they demand that their son divorce his wife. (*Ibn Umar*)

d. Nor if they ask him to hand over all his earnings to them.

e. If the parents take of their son's (or daughter's) property more than is sufficient for their genuine needs, it will be a debt in their account, which can be demanded back in this very life, and if it is not paid up here, they will be liable for it in the Hereafter. The commentary of the jurists (fuqaha) is enough for this. They understand its meaning very well, specially when they have the elucidated Tradition in Haakim to support them.

❖ ❖ ❖ ❖ ❖